Shobhit Mahajan teaches physics and astrophysics at the University of Delhi. He is also the Director of the Computer Centre at the Delhi University. He has a doctorate in physics from University of California, Berkeley, and has taught at St Stephen's College. He has written extensively on science and technology, and is the author of several books on science for children.

Shobhit lives in Delhi with his wife, son and a dachshund.

From Bugs to Black Holes

Discoveries that Changed the World

Shobhit Mahajan

PUFFIN BOOKS

PUFFIN BOOKS
Published by the Penguin Group
Penguin Books India Pvt. Ltd, 11 Community Centre, Panchsheel Park, New Delhi 110 017, India
Penguin Group (USA) Inc., 375 Hudson Street, New York, New York 10014, USA
Penguin Group (Canada), 90 Eglinton Avenue East, Suite 700, Toronto, Ontario, M4P 2Y3 (a division of Pearson Penguin Canada Inc.)
Penguin Books Ltd, 80 Strand, London WC2R 0RL, England
Penguin Ireland, 25 St Stephen's Green, Dublin 2, Ireland (a division of Penguin Books Ltd)
Penguin Group (Australia), 250 Camberwell Road, Camberwell, Victoria 3124, Australia (a division of Pearson Australia Group Pty Ltd)
Penguin Group (NZ), cnr Airborne and Rosedale Roads, Albany, Auckland 1310, New Zealand (a division of Pearson New Zealand Ltd)
Penguin Group (South Africa) (Pty) Ltd, 24 Sturdee Avenue, Rosebank, Johannesburg 2196, South Africa

Penguin Books Ltd, Registered Offices: 80 Strand, London WC2R 0RL, England

First published in Puffin by Penguin Books India 2005
Text copyright © Shobhit Mahajan 2005
Illustrations copyright © Penguin Books India 2005

All rights reserved

10 9 8 7 6 5 4 3 2 1

Typeset in Sabon by Mantra Virtual Services, New Delhi
Printed at Pauls Press, New Delhi

This book is sold subject to the condition that it shall not, by way of trade or otherwise, be lent, resold, hired out, or otherwise circulated without the publisher's prior written consent in any form of binding or cover other than that in which it is published and without a similar condition including this condition being imposed on the subsequent purchaser and without limiting the rights under copyright reserved above, no part of this publication may be reproduced, stored in or introduced into a retrieval system, or transmitted in any form or by any means (electronic, mechanical, photocopying, recording or otherwise), without the prior written permission of both the copyright owner and the above-mentioned publisher of this book.

For my father—an excellent storyteller
from whom I learnt so much,
without ever realizing it!

Contents

INTRODUCTION ix

THE BEGINNING OF TIME 1

WHY THINGS FLOAT 11

THE PRINTED WORD 18

THE NATURE OF THE UNIVERSE 25

THE FALLING APPLE 32

THE AGE OF STEAM 40

THAT DREAD DISEASE 48

THE SMALLEST WORLD 56

THE FIRST COMPUTER 63

THE AGE OF ELECTRICITY 70

THE AGE OF STEEL 77

THE DESCENT OF MAN 84

CALLING ACROSS THE MILES 92

THE AGE OF THE AUTOMOBILE 100

LET THERE BE LIGHT 108

THE INVISIBLE ENEMY 115

RULING THE AIRWAVES 121

SEEING WITHIN 129

THE MAGICAL MOULD 136

THE PARTICLES OF LIFE 143

Introduction

The one thing that distinguishes human beings from other animals is an insatiable curiosity about the natural world. And we are not just content to understand nature but also try to use it for our benefit. Whether it is the inhabitants of the Euphrates river valley domesticating wild grasses to start agriculture or Watson and Crick discovering the double helical structure of DNA—our curiosity and ingenuity is what distinguishes us from other creatures on earth.

This book is about human ingenuity—each of the twenty concepts, ideas or things which I have described in this book has played a major role in the progress of humankind. And they are examples of human creativity, intelligence, perseverance and, in some cases, serendipity. But that does not mean that these are the most important ideas or things in human history. Any such list is always subjective. Your choice would be somewhat different from mine.

Even for me, picking out twenty was very difficult. I struggled hard to leave out ideas like the Theory of Relativity or things like the transistor, the laser or even the humble magnetic compass, which made possible the long sea voyages which changed human history profoundly. My leaving these and other topics out of this book does not make them any less important—it is just that I had to choose twenty and the ones I have chosen reflect my own taste! The only thing that I can safely say is that these twenty are certainly important!

A word of thanks for Srijan and Nandita for being critical readers. And special thanks to my editor Sayoni Basu for being extremely cooperative and encouraging.

The Beginning of Time

Time: About 20,000 years ago. The earth is passing through an Ice Age. A group of nomadic hunters is resting in the cave that is their home for the moment, after a tiring hunt. As the sun sets, one of them picks up a stone and scratches a line on the cave wall. One more day is over. It has now been more than thirty days in this cave. It is time to move because it is becoming more and more difficult to find prey in this region.

Even the earliest humans noticed that certain events took place with great regularity—the rising and setting of the sun, the waxing and waning of the moon, the motion of the planets and the cycle of seasons. The sun, the moon and the stars have always provided us with a standard with which to measure the passage of time. The short passage of the day is measured by the sun, while the different phases of the moon provides another, longer standard of measurement. The regularity of natural phenomenon served humans well in marking lengths of time. The repetition of seasons first provided the idea of a year and the phases of the moon the idea of a month. Out of their observation of heavenly bodies and of the earth they lived on, humans devised calendars.

Calendars were important for agriculture, as humans moved slowly from being nomads to being farmers. Calendars were also used by the priests to organize rituals on auspicious days. The calendars gradually evolved in sophistication. Over thousands of years, ancient civilizations developed different calendars.

In almost all ancient civilizations, the counting of the days that constituted a year was done in similar fashion. Basically you look at some regular event, say the rising of the star Sirius or the sun, in line with a particular object, say a pyramid. If you count the number of days between the time that it takes for the event to recur, it comes to 365 days.

> Lunar calendars measure the months by using the cycle of full moon—new moon—full moon. Solar calendars measure the months from the sun going through thirty degrees in the sky (this corresponds to one zodiac sign or constellation since 360 degrees divided by twelve is thirty degrees).

The ancient Egyptians used a calendar of twelve months of thirty days each and then added five days at the end of the year to make up 365 days. These five days were considered unlucky to work and thus were a time for festivities.

The Sumerian calendar had twelve months of thirty days each. Each day consisted of twelve periods, and each period had thirty parts!

The ancient Greeks had a lunisolar calendar of 354 days. They were the first to intercalate extra months after specific number of solar years.

The Chinese calendar has twelve lunar months. As this leaves a discrepancy of eleven days in a year, they would add an extra month every 2.5 years.

> In India, the earliest known reference to a calendar is to a lunisolar (where the months are counted by the cycle of the moon but the year is reckoned by the motion of the sun) one in the *Rig Veda*.

We now know that the earth takes 365 days, five hours, forty-eight minutes and forty-six seconds to complete one revolution of the sun. As a result, the calendars devised by the ancients kept falling out of step with the motion of the earth. In fact, it might have also been that after hundreds of years, the mismatch was so much that winters in Egypt would come during the summer months!

There were many modifications to the calendar through the ages, as humans tried to keep up with the pace of the stars. A famous one was ordered by the Roman emperor Julius Caesar in 45 BCE. This was called the Julian calendar. It was more accurate than any of the contemporary ones, but it was still 11 minutes 30 seconds longer than the actual year. Though this seems a small amount, over hundreds of years, this small amount also adds up. For example, from 45 BCE to 1582, the discrepancy had become so much that the vernal equinox occurred ten days earlier than the traditional 21 March.

The Catholic Church modified the Julian calendar in 1582. This calendar is named after Pope Gregory XIII who ordered the reform. This is still in use today, with months being thirty or thirty-one days (except February, which is twenty-eight days) and every fourth year being a leap year.

> In India, the history of calendars is remarkably complex. In the 1950s there were about thirty major calendars in use in different parts of the country by different communities! After the calendar mentioned in the *Rig Veda,* advances in astronomy and the influence of Babylonian and Greek astronomy caused many changes to the calendar over the last two millennia. The Calendar Reform Committee set up by the government recommended a uniform calendar which is called the Saka era. The years are counted from the vernal equinox (22 March) 79 AD. The reformed calendar starts with Saka Era 1879, which corresponds to 22 March 1957.

Calendars have thus formed an important part of human history over the last 7000 years. This is still relatively recent, if we remember that the first humans walked the plains of Africa about a million years ago!

The earliest humans must have used the sun to order their 'day', which was the time between the rising and the setting of the sun. Depending upon the position of the sun in the sky, our ancestors could get an idea of the amount of daylight time left. Similarly, the motion of the stars in the sky at night would have served to indicate the passage of time. This rough and ready 'measuring' of time served humans well for several millennia. The reason for this was that life was simple, though hard. The day had to be spent in hunting, fishing, picking fruit, cooking and making tools, none of which required very precision timing.

With the start of agriculture some 10,000 years ago in what is now Middle East, humans began organizing themselves into larger societies. And as the society became more complex, the need for accurate time measurements was felt by people.

What is needed to make something a good and accurate timekeeper? All clocks—from the digital quartz Mickey Mouse watch that you are wearing to the primitive sundial—have two basic parts: a regular or repetitive process to indicate equal intervals of time and a way of keeping track of the change and displaying it. Thus, for instance, in the sundial, the passage of the sun across the sky provided the regular process while the length and position of shadow was a way to display the different times.

Around 3500 BCE the Egyptians constructed huge obelisks (pointed stone pillars) that were used as sundials. The shadow of the obelisk would move as the sun moved in the sky through the day. Once it was realized that one could use the position of the shadow to indicate time, more convenient sundials were made. You can see fairly accurate sundials at the Jantar Mantar in Delhi or in Jaipur.

The obvious disadvantage of sundials was that they could not work at night or even on cloudy days! To remedy this, the hourglass was constructed. No one knows how it was invented—possibly an idle man sitting and watching water drip from a hole in a tank had the idea of using it to measure time!

> You have undoubtedly noticed that the length of your shadow is different during different parts of the day. At noon, the shadow is the shortest because the sun is at its highest point. The shadows are longest in the morning and in the evening (though in opposite directions!). This simple fact can be used to mark time. If we use a fixed stick and mark the shadow position at different parts of the day, we can get a pretty good indication of the time. Of course, if one wanted the corresponding hours and minutes, one would have to first sit with a clock and mark the shadows on the hours.

The Egyptians used hourglasses. The tomb of the pharaoh Amenhotep I (buried around 1500 BCE) had one buried in it. The basic idea of the hourglass survived for a surprisingly long time. The Greeks began using it around 325 BCE and made several improvements to the basic design. However, the only time we use hourglasses today as are fancy egg timers or while playing Scrabble.

The next instrument devised to measure time was the mechanized water clocks. The water clock or clepsydra measured time by the flow of water through a small orifice. The time was marked usually on the sides of the container receiving the water, though sometimes it was also marked by the decrease in the level of the reservoir. Some water clocks also had floats, while others had a wheel which moved as the float moved down. The water clocks were possibly invented in Egypt but were also used in ancient Greece and Rome.

> In ancient Greece, the clepsydra was used to regulate the length of orations as well as speeches made in court.

There were water clocks that had fancy features, such as indicating the passage of time with doors opening (like modern-day cuckoo clocks). The Chinese made great advances in developing water clocks with more functions from 200 AD onwards. Around 1050 AD, a water clock tower about 30 feet high was built by Su Sung, an official of the Sung dynasty emperor, that had five front panels with doors and gongs to indicate the hours.

Water clocks had one major disadvantage—the flow of water is very hard to control accurately and so other methods of calculating time were needed.

For almost a thousand years—from 500 AD to 1500 AD—there was little development in the way time was measured. Of course, there were minor improvements in the design of water clocks and sundials. One major design change was the use of sand instead of water in a water clock. Another improvement was making really small sundials that could be carried in one's pocket, which was popular in the tenth century.

The major breakthrough came with the invention of mechanical clocks.

In the fourteenth century, the word clock came into existence. It comes from the French word *cloche*, which means bell. This was also the time when huge clock towers made their appearance in several Italian cities. These housed mechanical clocks that is used the fall of heavy weights. The essential idea in any mechanical clock or watch is that there has to be a source of energy that used to measure time. In the mechanical clocks of olden times (or even pendulum clocks like grandfather clocks), a falling weight provides the energy. The weight falls gradually, powering the pendulum which keeps time. When the weight is at its lowest position, it needs to be lifted up and the process starts again. Though very popular, these huge clocks were not very accurate because it was difficult to control the movement of the weights.

The Beginning of Time   7

> A fourteenth-century clock in Paris used a weight of more than 200 kilograms falling a distance of about 10 metres!

Around 1500, spring-powered clocks made their appearance in Nuremberg, Germany. Spring-powered clocks replaced the fall of the heavy weights by the unwinding of a coiled spring. The energy in these clocks was provided by coiling a spring. Remember the old watches which one had to wind every twenty-four hours? That is what wound the spring, which released its energy gradually, much like a gradually falling weight. These clocks were not very accurate but had the advantage of being small. They literally brought time into every home. You did not need to listen to the town clock tower to know the time; instead you could just look at your mantelpiece!

The clock that was both small in size as well as accurate was created in 1675 when Christian Huygens, a Dutch scientist, made the first pendulum clock. In the fifteenth century, Galileo, the famous Italian scientist who improved the design of the telescope to observe the planets and the stars, made experiments from the Leaning Tower of Pisa to study pendulums. He had noticed that the time taken for one oscillation or vibration of the bob was a constant, and based on this had sketched the design of a pendulum clock, which he never actually made. The clock made by Huygens used the regular motion of a pendulum to measure time and was very accurate for its day—it just lost one minute in a day!

Huygens made many further improvements to his clocks, including making a balance wheel and coiled spring arrangement that made possible portable clocks. The essential design of the watch that your parents used to wear is the same as what Huygens created! Of course there have been many developments which have made the watch more accurate and small. Hour, minute and second hands made their appearance around the eighteenth century. At about the same time, jewels were also used in the mechanism of the clocks. These reduced the friction in the bearings, and hence increased the life of the watch mechanism.

> Till the end of the sixteenth century, clocks had only an hour hand. In 1577, Jost Burgi invented the minute hand. This was part of a clock he designed for the famous Danish astronomer Tycho Brahe (1546–1601).

By the beginning of the twentieth century, watches had become very popular. Interestingly, only women usually wore wristwatches while men carried their watches in their pockets. During World War I, the soldiers realized that taking out a watch from the pocket was not particularly convenient when there was enemy fire all around. After that, wristwatches for men became more common.

> The famous French mathematician, Blaise Pascal (1623–1662) was the first person who is reported to have used a wristwatch. He attached a string to his pocket watch and put it on his wrist!

Wristwatches using springs were common till recently though another development around 1920 had made possible very much accurate clocks. This was the development of quartz crystals to keep time. Quartz is the second-most abundant mineral on our planet, found in most rocks and sand all over the world. Quartz crystals have a peculiar property where if you connect them to a battery, they change their shape. If you squeeze or bend the quartz crystal, it produces an electric current! This property, known by the complicated sounding name, piezoelectricity, is what lies at the heart of the Mickey Mouse watch that you are wearing.

The small battery in your watch powers tiny quartz crystals

The Beginning of Time 9

to vibrate at a fixed rate. And remember: as long as we have anything happening at a regular interval, we can use it to measure time. In this case, the passage of current in a quartz crystal makes it vibrate (change shape) at a fixed, fairly constant rate. If we can calibrate the vibration or rate of change in the shape of the quartz, we can use it to measure time.

The other thing needed is to display the time that in your quartz watch is done using small electronic bulbs called Light Emitting Diodes. Of course, all of this is done using very complicated electronic circuits. Quartz clocks and watches are extremely cheap and accurate for everyday use and hence are used by most people in the world now. The quality of the quartz crystal and the electronics inside the watch is what distinguishes a very expensive watch from a cheap one.

> Levi Hutchins invented the first alarm clock in 1787 in the US. But this clock could only sound the alarm at one fixed time, in this case at 4 a.m.!

Accurate though they are, quartz watches are not accurate enough for keeping standards of time. The frequency of vibration is not constant enough to serve as a standard against which clocks can be synchronized. Atomic clocks developed over the last fifty years have proved to be the most accurate timekeepers yet. Atomic clocks are based on the fact that every atom emits and absorbs light (or other radiation) at a characteristic frequency.

A simple example of this is sodium. Throw a pinch of salt on the gas stove in your kitchen and you will immediately see a yellowish glow in the flame. This is because the sodium in the salt (salt is a compound of sodium and chloride) when heated gives out its characteristic yellow colour or frequency.

Scientists have used this property to make a standard of

time. The most frequently used element is cesium. The first cesium atomic frequency clock was made in England in 1955. Atomic clocks are so accurate that in 1967, scientists decided to replace the definition of a second (which was traditionally in terms of the motion of the earth around the sun) to 9,192,631,770 cycles of a particular frequency of cesium!

Atomic clocks can be astoundingly accurate—the most accurate cesium clock has an error of 30 billionths of a second in one year! That might sound enough for you and me, but scientists are working on developing even more accurate atomic clocks.

Recently, scientists have made an atomic clock which is the size of a rice grain. This clock is about 10,000 times more accurate than the most accurate quartz clock and can be used in computers, mobile phones and other gadgets.

Many aspects of modern life depend on very accurate time such as airline autopilots to satellite navigation systems to power stations. If a person from ancient Egypt was to visit us now, he would be amused to see our lives so dependent on measuring time so accurately! But the way technology is progressing, we would feel the same if we were to be transported to the twenty-fifth century!

> In 1912, Warren Clock Company started producing a clock run by batteries, thus doing away with winding by hand.

Why Things Float

The Greeks had captured Syracuse around 700 BCE. By the third century BCE, Syracuse was the most powerful city in Sicily, and enormously wealthy. Its ruler was a man named Hieron. As befits a powerful and rich king, Hieron wanted a crown of pure gold. He asked a goldsmith to make him a beautiful gold crown in a very intricate design.

Some time later, the goldsmith brought him a crown that was truly a masterpiece. When Hieron tried it on, he looked like an emperor. The yellow gold shone in the morning light. The goldsmith was praised and rewarded for his work.

As often happened in the courts of kings, there were some people who were jealous of the goldsmith. Rumours soon spread that perhaps the goldsmith was not very honest. Some courtiers told the king that the goldsmith had fooled him and the crown was not made of pure gold.

This put Hieron in a difficult situation. On the one hand, he really liked the crown and did not want to destroy it to test the metal. On the other, he did not want to be cheated, particularly by one of his subjects, an ordinary goldsmith. How was he to verify that the crown was of pure gold without destroying the crown?

Among his courtiers was a wise man called Archimedes. He was a mathematician, scientist, astronomer and engineer. Hieron turned to him for a solution to this puzzle since Archimedes had in the past solved many tricky problems.

But this one stumped even Archimedes! He spent many

sleepless nights, trying to solve the puzzle but made no headway. There were many ways to ascertaining the volume of regular objects—such as cylinders, spheres and cubes, which would then make it possible to determine how much such an object should weigh if it was made of pure gold. But an irregular object like a crown?

The solution came to him in the most unlikely of all places—his bathroom! Deep in thought about the puzzle posed by Hieron, Archimedes stepped into his full bathtub, which promptly overflowed. This commonplace incident sparked off an idea.

According to legend, Archimedes was so excited by the idea that he jumped out of the bath and ran naked on the streets of Syracuse, shouting 'Eureka, eureka!', which is Greek for 'I have found it!' Of course, this sight of a naked man running down the streets did not amuse the people of Syracuse.

The solution that Archimedes found to the puzzle was what has come to be known as the Principle of Floatation, also called Archimedes's Principle after its formulator. This principle solved not only Hieron's puzzle but also explains how huge ships made out of iron manage to float in water while a piece of iron sinks.

All of us know that a piece of iron sinks in water while a piece of cork or paper floats. What is it that determines whether something is going to float or sink? The answer is something we all know instinctively, but maybe have never thought of it as a law of nature! We usually say that cork is lighter than water and hence floats, while iron is heavier and hence sinks. But what is the quantity that tells us that a particular object is lighter or heavier than something else? This quantity is called density and is basically the weight (or mass) of the object per unit volume. Water has a density of 1 gram per c.c. while iron has a density of around 7 gram per

Why Things Float

c.c. If the density of any object is more than 1 gram per c.c., it will not float.

So what was Archimedes's great bathtub insight? He realized that any body when immersed in a liquid is acted on by an upward force (called buoyancy) which is equal to the weight of the liquid it displaces. Or in other words, the body seems to lose weight when it is put in a liquid and the weight loss is equal to the weight of the liquid it displaces.

You have experienced all of these effects that Archimedes discovered while having a bath. When you swim, you feel lighter because of the apparent loss of weight that your body experiences. When you try and push a balloon in water, it seems to shoot upwards due to buoyancy. Archimedes's genius lay in generalizing from these everyday experiences to a universal law that is applicable everywhere and at all times.

How did this principle help Archimedes solve the puzzle posed by the king? Let us imagine that the crown weighed 3000 grams (a heavy crown, which would surely have given Hieron a pain in the neck!). Archimedes immersed it in water and weighed it. According to his principle, the crown will lose weight when in water and the loss in weight would be equal to the weight of water it displaces.

Let us say the crown weighed 2844 grams in water. Hence the loss in weight of the crown in water was 156 grams. Now since the density of water is 1 gram per c.c., 156 grams of water will occupy exactly 156 c.c. As the crown would be heavier than water and sink completely, it is clear that the volume of water displaced by the crown is also equal to its own volume.

Thus we now have the weight of the crown (3000 grams) and its volume (156 c.c.). We know that the density of a substance is its weight per unit volume which tells us that the density of the crown is simply 3000/156 = 19.3 grams per c.c. The density of pure gold, as Archimedes and his contemporaries would be familiar with, is 19.3 grams per c.c.

This simple demonstration immediately convinced Heiron that the crown was indeed made of pure gold, and that the goldsmith was an honest man. It is not clear what happened to the suspicious and scheming courtiers—maybe they were banished to another island to mine gold!

Archimedes's Principle is useful for many more things than catching unscrupulous goldsmiths. It actually allows us to understand how or rather why certain objects float or sink in liquids. The principle formulated by Archimedes is actually valid for all fluids as well, i.e., all liquids and gases. Thus, a parachute in air is as much governed by Archimedes's Principle as a ship sailing in the ocean.

Let us try and understand floatation now. After all, one of the puzzles that we think about is why a piece of iron sinks while a huge oil tanker floats in water. Let us imagine a very light substance, say a piece of cork. Now cork has a density of 0.175 grams per c.c. which, as we saw above, means that a cubic centimetre of cork weighs only 0.175 grams. (As a rough guide, a teaspoon typically holds about 5 c.c. of water.) Let us say that the cork has a volume of 10 c.c., i.e. it weighs 1.75 grams. Now what happens when I place this cork on water? We all know, the piece of cork floats on water. And why is that? Simple! Because Archimedes told us so!

What happens is that for a body to float, or in other words to be stationary in water, it must have no forces acting on it. This is something that we all see every day—when we apply a force to a body, it moves in the direction of the force. This simple observation forms the basis of another of the great laws of physics, called the laws of motion, which were first formulated by the great British scientist, Isaac Newton.

Let us return to our piece of cork placed in water. What

Why Things Float

are the forces acting on it? The one force that acts all the time on a body is the force of gravity, which pulls us towards the earth. And this force is such that the heavier the body, the more is the pull of gravity. In fact, the weight of the body can be taken to be a measure of the gravity force.

The cork weighs 1.75 grams, which is also the force of gravity pushing it down. Now if this was the only force on the cork, it will move down as it does if it was left in air. In water too, it starts moving down because of gravity.

But in water, it should also experience an upward force called buoyancy. This force is equal to the weight of water displaced. So as more and more of the cork is submerged under water, the buoyancy force increases because more and more water is being displaced. At this time, two forces are acting on the cork—the downward force of gravity, which is fixed, and an upward force of buoyancy, which increases as the cork gets submerged. Till such time as the gravity is more than the buoyancy, the cork keeps moving down, displacing more and more water, thus increasing the upward force. There comes a time when the two forces are equal. At that point, the cork stops moving and floats in water.

When does this happen? To balance the weight of cork (1.75 grams), the buoyancy force must be the same—that is, the weight of water displaced must be 1.75 grams. But 1.75 grams of water occupies only 1.75 c.c. and hence only 1.75 c.c. of cork will be submerged in water. Clearly, if the density of the object is higher, more and more of it will be submerged and of course, if the density of the object is more than 1 gram per c.c., it will sink in water.

Sounds simple, doesn't it? Actually, it is that simple—by Archimedes's Principle, we can also easily see why a huge ship does not sink. The ship is made of iron, which is, of course, heavier than water. In order to float, the ship needs to displace only its own weight of water.

Now the ship is not a mass of solid iron. It is hollow in large parts, and contains lots of air. In fact, the shape of a ship or a boat for that matter is precisely such that it includes a lot of air! If the ship was all iron, then of course, it would just sink.

Archimedes did much more than explain how objects float and sink in fluids. He is considered one of the most brilliant mathematicians and was also a great inventor of machines.

Archimedes was born in Syracuse in 287 BCE. Not much is known about his family, except that his father was an astronomer. It is believed that he studied in Alexandria in Egypt, which at that time was a famous centre for studying mathematics. Archimedes wrote several books on geometry, dealing with areas and volumes of figures and solids. He would be so intensely absorbed in his geometry calculations that he would neglect the chores of daily life. His servants had to forcibly take him to the baths. At the baths he would continue drawing diagrams on his oil-covered naked body!

> Among the most important contributions of Archimedes to mathematics was the proof that the volume of a sphere is two-thirds the volume of the cylinder that circumscribes the sphere. This is a problem that had baffled many ancient mathematicians. Archimedes was so proud of this solution that he had desired that this be depicted on his tomb.

Archimedes was better known in his times as a prolific inventor. He invented a pump called Archimedes' Screw when he went to Egypt. He also invented many war machines which helped Hieron in the war against the Romans in 212 BCE. In fact, the people of Sicily appreciated these machines much more than his work on pure mathematics! The war machines included a primitive missile system (a sort of catapult) and a system of mirrors to focus the sun's rays onto enemy ships.

Why Things Float

> One of the war machines made by Archimedes was called the Iron Hand or Archimedes's Claw. This machine used the principle of the lever (seesaw) and a lead counterweight to pull enemy ships out of water. Several engineers have recently made models of this machine. Among the most interesting one was a model of an Archimedes's Claw, built entirely of Lego bricks by Richard Wright in 1998.

'Give me a place to stand and I will move the earth,' Archimedes is reported to have said when he discovered the laws of levers and pulleys. To prove this, he was asked to move a ship which had required a large group of labourers to put into position. Archimedes did so easily by using a compound pulley system.

In 212 BC, the Roman army attacked Syracuse. Archimedes's war machines were very effective in defending the city. The Romans lost the battle but besieged Syracuse. Finally, the walls were breached and the Romans entered the city.

The Roman generals had been ordered to capture Archimedes alive. It is said that when the Romans entered the city Archimedes was so absorbed in some knotty problem that he had not registered their presence. A soldier asked Archimedes to come to the Roman camp but Archimedes refused to move until he had solved the problem. Outraged at this insolence, the soldier killed Archimedes.

Thus ended the life of one of the greatest thinkers of ancient times—about whom it is said that he was one of the greatest scientist and mathematicians of all times.

The Printed Word

The walled city of Dunhuang, on the north-western frontier of China, is small, sleepy and dusty. It used to be a very important town because it was the military base which guarded the famous Silk Route, the long highway connecting China with Central Asia. The Silk Route was possibly the most important trade route in the ancient world, as China was then one of the wealthiest and most technologically advanced countries in the world. From the beginning of the Christian era to about the fifteenth century, when the sea route to China was discovered, and most of the trade moved to ships, the Silk Route was taken by all traders and merchants across the heart of Asia.

Around 1900, an abbot named Wang Yuan-lu discovered stone grottoes in Dunhuang that were covered with sand. He began living in one of these caves and started the tedious process of clearing out the sand deposited in the others over several centuries.

One day, he was amazed to discover a secret library in one of the caves. The stone room contained nearly 10,000 manuscripts and silk scrolls. Hundreds of Buddhist monks must have spent their lives patiently copying these texts. Now they were lying in a room whose entrance had been bricked over and murals painted on it!

News of the discovery soon spread. In 1907, a British expedition led by Sir Aurel Stein visited Wang. Stein tricked the abbot into selling him twenty-four boxes of manuscripts and five boxes of paintings and other relics for £130!

The Printed Word

In one of the boxes was the *Diamond Sutra*, the world's earliest printed book. Made from seven strips of paper joined together with an illustration on the first sheet, the sixteen-feet-long scroll was printed in the year AD 868, a period when much of Europe was in the Dark Ages, thus named as there was no significant development in arts or science.

> You can visit the grottoes of Dunhuang, which yielded the first printed book. There are exquisite Buddhist frescoes there, and it is a major tourist attraction along the Silk Route.

The earliest form of 'printing' is possibly from ancient Babylon. Seals made in stone or clay were used for imprinting signatures and religious symbols. Several such seals have been discovered in the Harappan cities as well, and these were probably widely used in trade. The seal was usually dabbed with pigment or mud, and then pressed against any surface to make an impression. In such carved surfaces bearing text lay the origins of printing.

Manuscripts were copied by hand, using ink, a brush or even a quill pen in ancient Egypt and Greece, usually on papyrus, which was frail, and parchment made from sheep or goatskin. Works of literature, philosophy and science were copied by hundreds of slaves or monks, and distributed to those who could pay for it. As the process of copying was long and tedious, manuscripts were highly treasured and often very expensive. It was usually only religious or university libraries that had many books; even the richest individuals could not afford too many. As for the poor and middle class, there was no opportunity to own books.

> One of the earliest newspapers, the Roman *Acta Diurna*, is said to have been started by Julius Caesar.

But things were very different in ancient China. In AD 105,

Ts'ai Lun, a eunuch at the court of Emperor Ho Ti, made paper from the bark of the mulberry tree. Soon, paper was being made from rags as well as bamboo and other trees. The oldest known paper extant is from AD 150 and is made from rags.

The art of papermaking travelled to Japan around the beginning of the seventh century, and to Central Asia after another 150 years. By AD 800, paper was introduced in Egypt.

By the end of the second century AD, the Chinese had all the three elements needed for printing—paper, ink and carved surfaces bearing texts. No one knows exactly how they all came together. Maybe some devout pilgrim applied inked sheets of paper to marble pillars carved with the teachings of Buddha to transfer the text on to the paper.

By the fourth century, the Chinese had developed good-quality inks for printing. The spread of Buddhism in China expedited the process because of the Buddhist practice of making copies of sacred texts.

The next big step in printing came in China some time in the sixth century with the creation of the wood block. This allowed quick reproduction of the manuscripts for the first time. The text on a piece of paper was applied to a smooth piece of wood coated with rice paste. The ink in the paper would leave an impression on the rice paste. An engraver would then cut away the uninked areas so that the text stood out in reverse.

The wood block with the reversed text would be inked with a brush. A sheet of paper would be spread on it. When the paper was rubbed with a brush, the text on the block was transferred to the paper!

For centuries, hundreds of Buddhist texts, the teachings of the philosopher–sage Confucius, and scientific and mathematical texts were printed by this technique. The *Diamond Sutra* is the earliest surviving book made using wood blocks.

> The process for making a print from the block is similar to what you do when you want to transfer the Ashokan lion from a one-rupee coin on to paper. You take the coin, press a sheet of paper on it and use a soft pencil on the paper. Lo and behold, the impression on the coin is magically transferred to the paper!

While block printing resulted in quicker reproduction than copying manuscripts, it was still costly and time consuming. Each carved block could only be used for one page of the book. Making a whole book thus required carving hundreds of blocks of wood.

Around the eleventh century, a Chinese alchemist Pi Sheng thought of replacing the wood block with a movable type made from clay and glue. Each Chinese character was carved on a small block of moist clay. The clay was hardened by fire so that the character became hard and durable. Several such characters could be assembled to form words and sentences. They were put together on an iron plate which could be used to print a page.

Once the page was done, the characters (or type as they are called) could be reassembled to create other words and be used on another page, and so on. What Pi Sheng invented was the reusable type, an invention crucial to the development of printing.

Though block and reusable-type printing existed side by side in China for some time, the reusable type never really became very popular. The reason for this was the peculiar structure of the Chinese language. The Chinese alphabet does not function like the Roman or Hindi one you might be familiar with. Instead of letters adding up to make words, in the written form of Chinese, every word is assigned a character. Chinese written text consists of thousands of individual characters. To read an average newspaper, you need to know about 4000 characters. A good-sized dictionary would contain about 40,000 characters. This made the manufacture and assembling of type a very difficult process.

Marco Polo, the famous Venetian traveller who spent several years in China in the thirteenth century, saw the printed books there. It is possible that he brought back some to Italy. By this time, papermaking centres were flourishing in Italy, Germany and France.

Xylography, or the printing of books from wood blocks, also made its appearance in Europe around the fourteenth century. The availability of paper, which was better suited for reproducing the outlines from wooden blocks, made this easier. The manuscript copyists in the monasteries of Europe realized this and soon copies of religious works were made using wood-block printing. Some experiments with using reusable type with wood were also made in the early fifteenth century, which were unsuccessful. The letters of the Roman alphabet are much finer than the Chinese ideograms, and cutting them from wood was a delicate operation. The wood type created was fragile and wore out easily.

In the 1450s, there occurred an event which changed the whole course of human history. It was not that it was unprecedented—the developments around the world now make it seem inevitable that someone would do it. As it happened, the first printing press was set up by Johannes Gutenberg (1400–1468) in Mainz, Germany.

Little is known of Gutenberg's early life but he was possibly born in Mainz. He trained as a goldsmith and his family settled in the city of Strasbourg, where in 1438 he started his experiments in printing.

Gutenberg's contribution was to bring together technologies that were already in existence to make the first printing press. Paper was in use in Europe by Gutenberg's time, as was reusable ink. Unlike China and Japan, where most of the inks used were water soluble, the inks developed in Europe were oil-based.

The Printed Word

Gutenberg's true innovation lay in what he did with the type. He developed a punch and mould system that made possible the mass production of the movable type. His training as a goldsmith gave him much skill in the use of metals.

> In 1403, King Htai Tjong of Korea ordered a set of 100,000 pieces of type characters to be cast in bronze. Thus the Koreans actually invented the metallic moveable type from moulds. However, because their language was character-based like Chinese, it was found to be less practical than wood-block printing.

The first pieces of type were made by using a letter die in a soft metal like brass. Molten lead was then poured around the die to form a mould into which a mixture of lead, tin and antimony were poured. In this way, the movable type could be made easily and in large enough quantities. The letters were put together in a tray that was used to print a page. If any of the letters broke down, it could be easily replaced. When the page has been printed, the type could be disassembled and reused for another page.

The final piece of technology adapted by Gutenberg was the press. Screw-type presses had been used for centuries in Europe and Asia for pressing oil from olives or making wine from grapes. Gutenberg realized that this could be easily adapted to press a printing block on to a piece of paper. This was vastly superior to the brushing techniques that were used in China or Europe with wooden blocks, because the press made a much sharper impression and also allowed both sides of paper to be used.

With these innovations, Gutenberg was able to print, between 1450 and 1455, what is possibly the most famous book in the western world and what is known to us now as the Gutenberg Bible. The book took him over two years to print and it is still considered a masterpiece, considering the age in which it was printed.

As it happened, in 1455, Gutenberg had a falling out with his financier and partner, Johann Fust. As a result, Gutenberg lost his press and other equipment.

By 1460, he was bankrupt. He did set up another press and print other books, including another Bible. But his fortunes never really recovered and in 1467 or 1468, he died in penury in Mainz. The man whose ingenuity led to what has been called the single most important invention in the last two thousand years lies buried in an unknown church in that town.

The invention of the printing press occurred around the time that people like Galileo, Copernicus and Newton were questioning ancient and religious wisdom and developing scientific theories of the world. Around the same time, the German priest Martin Luther was bringing about a major reform in the Catholic Church. Gutenberg's printing press made possible for the first time, the availability of books for the general public. This helped in spreading the new ideas around Europe at an unimaginable speed.

The demand for printed books increased very rapidly. By far the biggest customer was the Church and most of the earliest publications were religious texts in Latin. By 1500, more than 6000 works had been printed, and the technology spread very fast throughout the world. By 1500, the city of Venice in Italy alone had over 400 printers! As early as 1539, barely forty years after Columbus accidentally landed in the Americas, a printing press was established in Mexico City. It was as if thousands of human beings had suddenly found a cheap and easy way to satisfy their hunger for knowledge!

The printed book quickly became extremely popular the world over. By 1501, there were over 1000 printing shops in Europe, which had produced 20 million copies of 35,000 titles.

The Nature of the Universe

24 May 1543. An old man lay on his deathbed in the small town of Frauenburg in Poland. He had spent almost fifteen years of his life writing a book on astronomy called the *De Revolutionibus Orbium Coelestium* (*On the Revolutions of the Celestial Spheres*). It was as he lay dying that Nicolaus Copernicus received the first published copy of his book.

It was a book that was to change the way we, human beings, thought of ourselves in the universe. It could be said to be among the most influential books of all times.

Human beings have always wondered about the universe. Even before the dawn of so-called civilization, tribal and nomadic societies had their own theories of how the universe began, what there was in it, and what our place is in the grand scheme of things. The sight of the night sky with its thousands of twinkling stars and the shining moon inspired wonder and gave rise to stories about the things in the sky. Awe-inspiring events like eclipses of the sun and the moon terrified people. The daily motion of the sun in the sky during the daytime and that of the moon during the night, the cycle of the seasons—all these led people to conjecture about the nature of the universe.

Almost every ancient civilization had its own interpretation of the nature of the universe. The great Greek philosopher, Aristotle (384–322 BCE), wrote several books on the heavens (as the sky was usually called). In his books *On the Heavens* and *Physics*, he put forward a theory of a very ordered universe, divided into two parts—the earthly region and the heavens. The earthly domain, which was the centre of the universe, is where we lived and this was constantly changing; things were born, grew old and died. But in the heavens everything was perfect and unchanging, and made up of a substance called æther. The heavenly bodies were all part of eight concentric, spherical shells that fitted tightly around each other. These were the moon, Mercury, Venus, the sun, Mars, Jupiter, Saturn and the fixed stars beyond Saturn. These shells moved in a circular orbit around the earth. The motion was controlled by the Prime Mover from beyond the shell of the fixed stars.

This theory was aesthetically satisfying—everything was spherical and in perfect order. The only problem was that it did not match what people saw in the sky! The Greeks could see that objects in the sky speeded up, slowed down and, in the case of the planets, even seemed to reverse their motion.

> It was not that the planets actually reversed their motion, but sometimes it looked as if they had. If the planets were revolving in circles around a stationary earth, this would not be possible. The real reason is that the planets, as well as the earth, are moving in well-defined orbits around the sun. Thus, against a background of fixed stars (fixed because they are so far away that the earth's motion around the sun doesn't change their positions in the sky), the paths of the planets change depending on their relative positions with respect to the earth.

This reverse or retrograde motion puzzled the Greek philosophers greatly. If the planets moved in perfectly circular orbits at a fixed speed, there is no way one can explain how they could slow down or reverse their direction.

This was not the only problem with Aristotle's theory. The planets, especially Mars, Venus and Jupiter, showed varying brightnesses, which we know today is because they are at varying distances from earth due to their elliptical orbits around the sun. When they are closer, they look brighter. However, since in the Aristotelian theory, planets are supposed to be at fixed distances from the earth and move in perfectly spherical orbits, it was logically impossible for them to vary in brightness.

So great was the prestige of Aristotle that it was only some five hundred years later, around the second century AD, that other philosophers acknowledged the deficiencies of Aristotelian theory by trying to modify it. Among them was Ptolemy who, in his massive book *Almagest*, did not overturn the perfect order as proposed by Aristotle but modified it slightly so that the phenomenon actually observed in the sky was explained. Instead of just spherical shells of planets and stars, he introduced smaller circles called epicycles. The planets moved along these smaller circles, whose centres in turn moved on the spherical shell around the earth. The different positions of the planets on the epicycles at different points in time was the reason why planets vary in brightness.

Ptolemy's model of the universe lacked the perfect symmetry and order of the Aristotelian universe. However, it did have the advantage of being able to explain the observations. But many people continued to abide by the earlier theory. Until the thirteenth century, there was a peculiar situation in Europe. Philosophers and the Church swore by Aristotle's universe, while those interested in astronomy, astrology and calendar-making used Ptolemy's theory!

Nicolaus Copernicus was born in 1473 in Torun in eastern Poland. Copernicus's father was a wealthy merchant and his mother also belonged to a wealthy family. Copernicus spent his childhood in Torun. After he entered the University at Krakow in 1491, he became fascinated by astronomy, an interest that stayed with him till his death. Copernicus never got a degree from the university though he studied there for four years.

Copernicus's uncle was the bishop of Ermeland and wanted Copernicus to enter the canonry of Frauenburg as a church administrator so that he would get enough money to carry out his intellectual pursuits. The job involved handling the finances of the Church but had no religious responsibilities. As it happened, there was no vacancy in the church at that time, and so his uncle sent him to Italy to study medicine and law.

In 1497, Copernicus joined the University of Bologna, one of the oldest universities in the world. He stayed in the house of a mathematician, Domenico Maria de Novara. Domenico Maria was one of the few people in Europe at that time who were critical of the Ptolemaic theory of the universe. It is almost certain that Copernicus's astronomical interests were greatly stimulated by his host. He also spent some years at the University of Padua.

After getting a degree in law, Copernicus returned to Poland in 1503 and started assisting his uncle, the bishop. After his uncle's death in 1512, Copernicus moved to Frauenburg where he stayed for the rest of his life.

> The first book written by Copernicus was a Latin translation of Greek verses on ethics by a seventh-century Byzantine poet, published in 1509. He also wrote a book on money and currency in the 1520s but this was not published till 1816.

Having studied in some of the major centres of learning in Europe, Copernicus was well aware of the existing knowledge in mathematics, astronomy and medicine. It was his medical training that was most useful to him because he frequently treated various members of the clergy, and thus undoubtedly gained influence in the Church.

Meanwhile, Copernicus continued his study of astronomy. His dream was a systematic programme of observations of the heavens to be able to understand the Ptolemaic system.

Unfortunately, it seems he was never able to fulfil this desire. But he was able to get enough information for him to calculate the orbits of the sun, moon and planets around the earth. The more he studied the heavens, the more he was dissatisfied with the complicated Ptolemaic system of explaining it. He became convinced that a simpler explanation of the planetary motion was possible. To this end, he started reading the works of some of the Greek philosophers.

He was surprised to find that the idea that the earth is not at the centre of the universe had actually been proposed by some Greeks but had never gained popularity. Copernicus now started working on this idea and, after several years of painstaking calculations, found that this idea did indeed account for the observations. He worked on preparing a short book with his new ideas from 1510 to 1514. This book, which he circulated privately among his friends, contained the kernel of his theory. From 1514 to 1530, he worked on a longer, more detailed analysis, which was eventually to become *On the Revolutions of the Celestial Spheres*, but did not have enough courage to print it!

> The Church was obviously impressed by Copernicus the astronomer because he was invited in 1514 to give his opinion on calendar reform. He refused to express any opinion because he felt that the positions of the sun and the moon were not known accurately enough for him to make any statement on the correctness of the calendar!

Why was Copernicus so scared of publishing his ideas? The reason lay in the fact that his ideas were turning 1500 years of established knowledge on its head! And worse, they were not in agreement with what the Church believed. The Catholic Church was the most powerful institution in Europe in those days. It required a lot of courage for anyone to go against what the Church propagated. As an official of the

Church, for Copernicus to publicize his heretical views was unthinkable.

What was so revolutionary about Copernicus's theory? The main tenet was that it was the sun, and not the earth, that was at the centre of the universe. The daily motions of the sun and the stars, the planets and the seasons, could all be explained if we took the sun to be at the centre of the universe and the earth to rotate on its axis and revolve around the sun. This theory, called the heliocentric theory (from the Greek *helios*, which means sun), now ordered the planets according to their distances from the sun. Mercury, Venus, Earth with the moon orbiting around it, Mars, Jupiter, Saturn and then the fixed stars made up the heavens in his view.

> Copernicus could not get himself to abandon the beauty of planets moving at a fixed speed in circular orbits around the sun! In the early seventeenth century, another astronomer, Johannes Kepler, ultimately propounded that planets move in elliptical orbits.

Though the Copernican theory contained many flaws, it was still a major step for humankind. For one, it increased the scale of our universe many times from what was previously thought. If the stars are fixed on a shell at the limit of the cosmos, as the earth moved in a circle around the sun, we should be seeing the stars move too. Just as we see trees moving backwards as we travel forward in a moving car, the stars should also show some motion as the earth moved. But this is not what we observe. The only possible explanation is that the stars are so far away that our motion makes no difference in their positions. To continue the car metaphor, this is just like when we observe a faraway tree from a car. If the tree is really far away, it seems to move much more slowly than the car itself. Thus, the fact that we do not see the stars move would imply that they are much further away than was previously thought. The universe was thus much bigger than was imagined earlier.

More importantly, in one stroke Copernicus had removed human beings from the centre of the universe to an insignificant position among the other heavenly bodies. We may not think this to be very significant now, but at that time, this was a remarkable change in thinking. According to the Bible, man was God's special creation, at the very centre of the universe. Copernicus destroyed this notion.

Copernicus was most reluctant to publish his book because he realized that this would lead to a conflict with the Church. He was nevertheless persuaded to publish it by his pupil, Georg Rhaticus. In 1540, Rhaticus took the manuscript to Germany to find a printer. After much difficulty he found one who was willing to publish it, Andreas Osinder in Leipzig. But Osinder was also nervous about the response the book might provoke. He inserted a preface claiming that the hypothesis that the sun was at the centre of the universe was only a means for calculating the planetary orbits and had nothing to do with reality! It was this copy that Copernicus finally saw on the day of his death in 1543.

> The Church did not easily accept the Copernican theory. *On the Revolutions* was banned as heretical till 1835!

But despite this preface, there were enough courageous scientists who took the Copernican theory seriously. Among them was an Italian astronomer called Galileo Galilei. He used the newly invented telescope to study the heavens and was convinced that Copernicus was right. Galileo had to suffer immensely for expressing this view—opposing the Church was not easy in those days. Galileo's work was banned in the seventeenth century, and it was not until 1992 that the Church officially acknowledged its error!

The Falling Apple

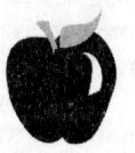

Between April 1665 and October 1666, about 100,000 people died in London and other parts of south-east England. The reason for this devastation was a deadly epidemic, the bubonic plague. The Great Plague, as it came to be known, made many people flee to the countryside from cities. The king and his court left London. And Cambridge University was temporarily closed.

As all the students at Cambridge were forced to go home, young Isaac Newton returned to his mother's house at Woolsthrope in Lincolnshire. He spent the next two years there, thinking about nature and its workings. The famous story about an apple falling on Newton's head happened at this time. The story may be false but what is certainly true is that Newton, in these two years, changed science beyond all recognition.

Over a century earlier, Copernicus and later Galileo had shaken the foundations of our view of the heavens with the heliocentric theory. A few decades later, German astronomer Johannes Kepler was painstakingly studying the observations of the heavens taken over a period of twenty years by Danish astronomer, Tycho Brahe. Kepler realized that the Copernican theory was correct in assuming that the sun was at the centre of the cosmos but wrong in thinking of planets moving at a fixed speed in circles around it. His observations convinced him that planets actually moved in elongated circles or ellipses around the sun and that their speed varied along the orbit.

The Falling Apple

Why this happened was unknown, though Kepler had hinted at some kind of force that caused this motion.

This was the state of our knowledge about the heavens in 1642 when two things of immense significance to modern science happened—Galileo died and Newton was born.

Newton's father was a rich farmer who died three months before his son was born. His mother remarried when he was two and Isaac was sent to live with his grandmother in Woolsthorpe. Newton was treated like an orphan and had a very unhappy childhood. He attended a nearby school and showed no promise at all. His teachers commented that he was very quiet, idle and inattentive in school. But he was very good with his hands, and made models of windmills, solar dials and other contraptions.

In 1661, Newton's mother was persuaded by his former schoolteacher and an uncle to arrange to admit him to Trinity College, Cambridge. Newton had wanted to study law, but ended up studying mathematics and astronomy. He got his bachelor's degree in 1665. And then the plague started and Newton had to return to Woolsthorpe for over two years.

> Newton had a very bad temper and suffered frequent nervous breakdowns. One such breakdown occurred when the German mathematician Gottfried Wilhelm Liebniz claimed that he had first thought of the theory of calculus. The actual historical position is not very clear but nowadays both of them are jointly recognized as founders of calculus.

The countryside offered few distractions. Newton spent most of his time thinking about mathematics and astronomy. In this period, he laid the foundations of a new branch of mathematics which we now call calculus, and which deals with concepts such as rate of change of quantities, the maximum and minimum value of quantities and areas bounded by curves.

Calculus was immensely useful to Newton in solving complicated problems, especially those regarding the orbits of planets. And it was as Newton was wondering what kind of force kept the moon in its orbit around the earth, that the apple allegedly fell from a tree, making him realize that the reason for both the apple falling and the moon orbiting the earth were the same—the pull of gravity!

Newton proposed that any two bodies in the universe attract each other with a gravitational force. This force depends on the distance between the two bodies and on the masses of the bodies. It decreases with the distance (as the square of the distance) and increases with the mass. Thus two 1-kilogram masses placed one metre apart will attract each other with four times the force of gravity than if they were placed two metres apart. On the other hand, a 2-kilogram mass will have twice the attraction of a 1-kilogram mass at the same distance.

> Newton was not the first to have been troubled by the falling of bodies to the earth. The ancient Greek philosophers had several theories about it. Aristotle thought that all things were made of four elements: earth, fire, water and air. Similar objects attracted one another while dissimilar ones repelled. Thus, objects with earth in them fell to the ground while fire rose up! Galileo also worked on falling of objects and concluded that all objects fell to the earth with the same acceleration.

This was a very profound discovery. While others had speculated about gravity, Newton's genius lay in connecting this simple, everyday happening with something totally different—the orbit of the moon. And in this process, he formulated a universal law, one that was valid everywhere and at all times. Newton did not really pursue his studies on gravity at this time, but spent his time working on calculus and the properties of light.

The Falling Apple

Newton returned to Cambridge in 1666. The following year, he was elected a fellow of Trinity College, and in 1669 the Lucasian Professor of Mathematics at Trinity College. During this time, Newton's work was in mathematics, mostly calculus, and the nature of light. He made some very important discoveries about the properties of light, including showing that sunlight is made up of seven colours. Another area he devoted much attention to was formulating the laws of motion.

Recognition started coming Newton's way. He was elected a Fellow of the Royal Society in 1672 and his fame spread all over Europe. As his work became well known, there was a lot of criticism of his ideas from some scientists. In fact, a well-known English scientist, Robert Hooke, claimed that Newton had borrowed his ideas on gravitation!

In 1679, Newton returned to applying his theory of gravitation to the orbits of planets. By 1680, he had shown that it was indeed under the influence of the sun's gravity that the planets moved in orbits as proposed by Kepler.

Newton started compiling his work on gravity and the motion of the planets. He spent the next seven years working out a complete theory of gravity and motion which he published as *Philosophiae Naturalis Principia Mathematica*. This book is considered one of the most influential books of the last thousand years! It was a tremendous achievement for any one human being to bring together in an orderly fashion a complete theory of gravity and motion.

Newton's laws of motion are equally fundamental to our understanding the world around us. The three laws now known by his name form the cornerstone of modern-day physics.

Newton's first law is a statement of the principle of inertia. This might sound like a big word but is essentially saying what we see every day. Imagine going in a car on a smooth road. All of a sudden a boy runs across the road and the driver applies his brakes suddenly. What happens? We tend to keep on moving and usually hit the windscreen if we are not wearing our seatbelts! Or think about what happens when the car starts from rest. As soon as it starts, we are thrown back. In both these cases, it is as if we do not want to change our state of rest or motion. This is what Newton's first law is all about. All bodies tend to move uniformly in a straight line unless acted upon by a force. On a more practical level, rockets, once they are outside the gravitational pull of the earth, continue to move in a straight line without firing their engines because there are no forces to prevent them from continuing their motion.

The second law of Newton is also well known to us by experience. It states that any force acting on a body causes an acceleration. This acceleration depends on the force and the mass of the body. The larger the force, the more the acceleration. On the other hand, for the same force, the larger the mass, the smaller the acceleration. Thus it is easier to push a small stone than a large rock. In our everyday experience though, the force of friction between the objects complicates things a bit!

Newton's third law is the well-known statement that every action has an equal and opposite reaction. Once again, we see this law in operation all around us. If we light a rocket on divali, why does it go up? Simple, because Newton said so! Actually what happens is that the chemicals burning inside the rocket push out gasses at a very high speed. Now the rocket pushes out gas backwards (action) and so the rocket gets pushed forward (reaction). This is the same principle used in spacecrafts and missiles. Of course, there the gasses are pushed out at extremely high speeds (the velocity needed to escape the gravitational pull of any astronomical body is known as escape velocity) to provide enough force to the

The Falling Apple

spacecraft for it to be able to escape the earth's gravity. Newton once again!

> The escape velocity from the gravitational pull of any astronomical body depends on the mass or weight of the body, and its size. Thus, for instance, the escape velocity from earth is about 11 km/sec while that from the surface of the moon is only 2.4 km/sec! On the other hand, escaping from the gravity of the heavyweight giant Jupiter one needs to be moving at more than 60 km/sec!
>
> Suppose that there is an object whose mass is so huge and its size so small that the escape velocity is the speed of light! What happens in that case? Light travels at a blazing 300,000 km/sec—and nothing can move faster than light. In 1800, a famous French astronomer Laplace talked about small, very dense and heavy astronomical bodies which would have such high escape velocities.
>
> Imagine standing on such a body and shining a torch upwards—the light from the torch would come right back at you since it is not moving fast enough to escape from the body! It would be just like your throwing a stone upwards and it returning right back at you because the speed of the stone is not large enough to escape the earth's gravity!
>
> For a long time, Laplace's ideas remained speculative but we now know that there are indeed such dark beasts in the universe which are so small and dense that not even light can escape from them. Such objects are called black holes and are truly amongst the most amazing objects in our universe. A typical black hole can have twice the mass of our sun but have a size of only about 5 km!

After the publication of the *Principia*, Newton was widely acknowledged to be the greatest scientist in the world. But along with fame came criticism, including more charges of plagiarism. Newton suffered a nervous breakdown in 1693 and retired from research. In 1696, he decided to leave Cambridge and take up the job of the Warden of the Royal Mint.

> Newton's personal life was always troubled and disturbed. He spent his childhood virtually like an orphan. He never married, and led an extremely lonely existence, finding solace in theology and religion.

Newton took his job at the mint seriously and initiated many measures to prevent counterfeiting of coins. He introduced coins of standard weights as well as coins with milled edges. Soon he was promoted to be the Master of the Mint, a job that made him very wealthy and which he continued to keep until his death.

From time immemorial, people have tried to change base metals like lead and iron into gold. Newton too was very interested in alchemy, and tried several experiments to transform metals. It is thought that his frequent nervous breakdowns might have been the result of his inhaling poisonous chemicals during his alchemic experiments! In the later part of his life, he spent most of his time on his experiments with alchemy and in trying to find the accurate dates of Biblical events.

In 1703, Newton was elected the President of the Royal Society, and in 1705 was knighted by Queen Anne, the first scientist to be so honoured. He continued to publish his work, including *Optiks,* which contained all the work Newton had done on the properties of light.

> Newton was the first person to have used a prism to split sunlight into its constituent seven colours. He also developed a theory of colour.

His health started to fail and he died in 1727, in Kensington near London. After his death, he was buried in Westminster Abbey, once again being the first scientist to be so honoured. After his death, it was found that his body had a very large amount of mercury, possibly from his alchemic pursuits!

The Falling Apple

Newton can be thought of as the single most important figure in modern science. His work on gravity, motion and optics would alone make him great. But it was the method used by Newton which has found applications in all branches of modern science, which truly makes him the father of modern science. He was a pioneer in the use of mathematics to the study of nature. His theory of gravitation was an example of how one principle could explain very different natural phenomena.

The Age of Steam

On a fine Sunday afternoon, early in 1765, an instrument maker at the University of Glasgow was taking a walk on the park near his shop. Though he was enjoying the uncharacteristically good weather, his mind dwelled on a problem that had been posed to him by a professor at the university.

The university had a model of a steam pump designed several decades ago by Thomas Newcomen. This pump was not working properly. Twenty-nine-year-old James Watt had realized what was at fault. But he had not been successful in finding a solution.

During the course of Watt's walk, an idea suddenly struck him. He was convinced that he could not only fix the Newcomen pump but also improve on it considerably. This germ of an idea was the beginning of the Age of Steam. Watt's design of the steam engine was responsible for its widespread use in industry and transportation, which eventually led to the Industrial Revolution.

Watt wanted to work on his idea immediately. But it was Sunday, the Day of the Lord. It was customary not to work on that day. He waited impatiently for Monday morning.

The following morning, Watt rushed into his shop and immediately got to work. He tested his idea with the help of a makeshift apparatus and was thrilled to realize that it worked. However, it would still take more than a decade for his revolutionary idea to be put into practice.

The Age of Steam

> You may have heard the story about Watt watching the tea pot boil in his mother's kitchen when he was a boy, and from that getting the idea of a steam engine. Like Newton and his apple, we do not know whether there is any truth in that story.

Contrary to what is generally believed, Watt did not invent the steam engine. The idea of the steam engine is a very old one. The first mention we find of the use to steam to perform a mechanical task is in the writings of Hero of Alexandria, a Greek who lived around the first century AD. He describes a contraption by which the gates of a temple could be opened when the lamps at the altar were lit. The heat produced steam in a vessel of water kept underneath, which operated a pulley system to open the doors. The mechanism to do so was cleverly hidden under the floors, so that it seemed as if the doors opened by magic. No doubt, the worshippers at the temple would have been deeply impressed by the powers of the priests, who could open doors at a distance, and the priests would not have revealed the mechanism as the mystic aura added to their prestige!

Several other people toyed with the idea of using steam to perform some useful work. The first recorded practical use of steam came with the pump designed by the French inventor Denis Papin in 1690. Papin's engine was used to pump water but was little more than a curiosity because it was too crude to be of real use.

In 1698, the English engineer Thomas Savery built a pump that was a considerable improvement on Papin's engine. Savery's engine was used to remove water from coalmines, which previously had required an elaborate system of buckets, pulleys and a team of horses. This was the first truly impressive demonstration of the power of steam. It had taken human beings several millennia to find a substitute for animal power for doing useful work.

Savery's engine was not very sophisticated. It could only pump water from shallow depths and would frequently explode. Nevertheless, he cleverly took out a very broad patent on it.

In 1712, John Newcomen, a blacksmith by training, built the first truly practical steam engine after ten long years of work. This could be used to remove water from the mines more efficiently. He was forced to collaborate with Savery because of the latter's patent and thus possibly lost out on making a lot of money from his invention!

Newcomen's engine, though a tremendous improvement on previous designs, suffered from various faults. But since this was the only one available, it was used fairly extensively in mines. It was working on Newcomen's engine that had made Watt devise his immensely more sophisticated engine in 1765.

Watt was born in 1736 in Scotland. His father was a carpenter who worked in the shipbuilding industry. Watt was a sickly child, frequently suffering from migraines and toothaches! He enjoyed mathematics at school and also learnt a lot about carpentry from his father at home. Watt was fascinated by the various instruments used in navigation of ships and decided to become an instrument maker.

This was easier said than done. Unlike today, where one can learn these skills at colleges, the only way to learn the trade in those days was to be an apprentice to an instrument maker. This meant several years of hard labour with little pay in what were frequently terrible conditions. Watt finally managed to get an apprenticeship. He so impressed his master with his skills that the master agreed to reduce the period of learning from seven years to one.

Watt started working at a feverish pace since he wanted to learn all he could in that one year. He worked long hours in the cold workshop, living on a small sum of money sent

The Age of Steam

by his father and eating very little. By the end of the year, his health declined severely but his enthusiasm was still intact.

> During the time that Watt was an apprentice, England was at war with France. The state was looking for able-bodied men to serve in the army. Watt spent most of his time indoors in his workshop to avoid being forcibly conscripted by the army.

In 1756, Watt, now a trained instrument maker, returned to Glasgow and was appointed the mathematical instrument maker at the University of Glasgow. It was here that he got interested in the steam engine.

What exactly it was that Watt did can only be understood if we know how the steam engines before Watt worked. All steam engines work on the principle that the energy of steam, produced on heating water, can be transformed into mechanical energy. This mechanical energy can be used to run trains or electrical generators or even open temple doors! In a steam engine, this transfer of steam energy to mechanical energy is done by allowing the steam to expand and cool in a cylinder to which is attached a movable piston. Think of a syringe which your doctor uses to give you a tetanus injection when you fall from your bicycle. The syringe has a plunger which moves in a glass (or plastic) cylinder. This is exactly what an engine has—the piston is like a plunger and it moves up and down.

Newcomen's engine had a vertical cylinder fitted with a piston which was attached to a counterweight, which would pull it down. Steam produced in a boiler was let into the bottom of the cylinder to fill it. The piston moved to the top because of the pressure of the steam. A jet of cold water was sprayed on the cylinder. This caused the steam to condense. As the steam turned into water, the pressure in the cylinder decreased, creating a vacuum of sorts. The air pressure outside the cylinder now pushed the piston to the bottom of the cylinder. This up-and-down motion of the piston was used to drive a pump to pull water. In this engine, the steam is not actually pushing the piston; it is air pressure that does the actual work.

Newcomen's engine was terribly inefficient because the cylinder has to heat and cool repeatedly. This not only increased the cost of fuel used to heat water, but the continuous fluctuations in temperature also caused the cylinder to explode frequently.

Watt realized what the problems with the Newcomen engine were. However, solving them was another thing altogether. As he pondered on it during his walk that fateful Sunday, it suddenly struck him that a separate condensing chamber could be used to cool the steam. This condensing chamber would greatly increase the efficiency of the engine because the cylinder would not have to be alternately heated and cooled. His tests that following Monday morning showed that the model worked. Making an actual engine where this model could be commercially used would prove to be far more difficult.

The first difficulty was to find a person who was ready to fund such an enterprise. But Watt was fortunate—he met industrialist John Roebuck who agreed to finance the development after he saw the model work.

Over the next four years, Watt tried hard to construct a working engine based on this design. Though he made several engines, none of them worked satisfactorily. Most people would have abandoned the project at this stage. But Watt kept on trying even after the experiments failed.

In 1769, Watt obtained the patent on his design. Roebuck financed Watt and paid off his debts in return for two-thirds share in all the money that the invention might make. Watt thought this was very reasonable, especially since no success was in sight.

The years of toil left their mark however. Watt became disheartened and abandoned his experiments to start doing survey work for canal building.

In 1773, Roebuck's financial situation took a turn for the worse. As a result, he sold off his interest in Watt's patent to Matthew Boulton, an industrialist Watt had met earlier and who had immediately recognized the potential of Watt's ideas. Watt started work again on his engine at Boulton's factory where there were many skilled artisans to help him.

> Watt was a modest and shy man. He once wrote to Boulton, 'I would rather face a loaded cannon than settle a disputed account or make a bargain'!

In 1776, eleven years after that Sunday walk, the first Boulton–Watt engine was demonstrated in a mine. It worked just like Watt had thought it would! This engine was to change the face of England and the rest of the world.

Watt's design had increased the efficiency of steam engines considerably. Unlike the engines before it, it used steam pressure instead of air pressure to do the work. But to use the engine for anything other than pumps required a mechanism where the piston's motion could be turned into a rotary motion to drive machinery. Although Watt's motive was to make machinery move, his design of the crankshaft was what made possible the steam locomotive. If you see a steam train engine today, you can still see Watt's crankshaft attached to the wheels.

By 1800, close to a hundred cotton mills in Britain used Watt's engine to run their machinery. By this time, Watt had patented several other inventions such as the double-action engine in which steam entered alternately from both ends of the engine, and the steam indicator which recorded the pressure inside an engine. He retired from the company that he had started with Boulton to devote more time to his research.

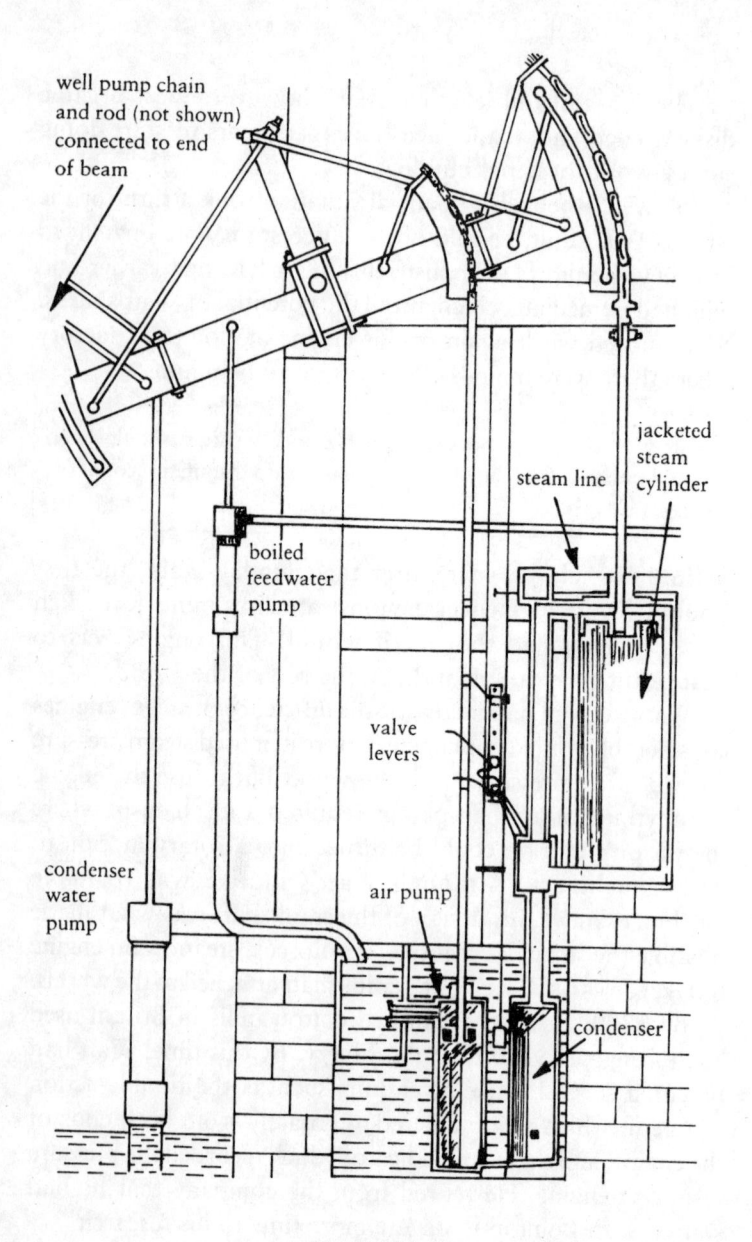

Watt's Engine

The Age of Steam

> Among Watt's many inventions was the speed governor which automatically regulated the speed of the engine by controlling the amount of steam entering it. This was the first use of the principle of feedback where the output is linked to the input. This concept is fundamental to automation in our own times.

By the beginning of the nineteenth century, Watt was wealthy and famous. His invention was the catalyst for England's rapid industrialization which would lead to the Industrial Revolution as it made mass manufacturing possible.

By the time Watt died in 1819, the steam engine had been used to drive a locomotive. In 1804, a British inventor, Richard Trevithik demonstrated the first practical locomotive using a steam engine. In 1819, a locomotive named Rocket was designed by George Stephenson. It pulled a load three times its own weight at a speed of about 20 kilometre/hr. After this, the growth of the railways was tremendous. Within a few years, hundreds of miles of railway lines were laid in England and other countries. The growth of the railways provided further impetus to the Industrial Revolution as raw materials could now be moved swiftly and cheaply. Equally important was its impact on human transportation.

Watt was not the first person to think about the power of stream and create the steam engine. His achievement lies in making an engine which allowed the power of steam to be harnessed efficiently. Though steam locomotives have now been almost totally replaced by diesel and electric trains, steam ruled the railways for more than a century.

That Dread Disease

In May 1796, a dairymaid named Sarah came to see a doctor in the small town of Berkeley in Gloucestershire, England. The doctor was well known in the area as one who was not only a good surgeon but also a caring human being.

Sarah had developed a rash on one of her hands and was very scared that it might be the dreaded smallpox. Edward Jenner reassured her and diagnosed the rash as cowpox. Sarah confirmed that one of her cows, called Blossom, had had cowpox recently and it was possible that she had contracted it from the cow during her milking.

Most doctors at the end of the eighteenth century were content with using time-tested techniques and medicines to treat their patients. There was not very much quest for research or new medicines. Edward Jenner, however, was not one of them. He had heard people in the countryside claiming that those who had had cowpox do not catch smallpox. But while most doctors dismissed this as bunkum, Jenner wanted to test the theory himself.

For most of us, who are fortunate in that we have never seen a case of smallpox in our lives, it is difficult to imagine the dread that the disease caused. Smallpox is an ancient disease. The Egyptian pharaoh Rameses V got the disease as is evident from the pockmarks on his mummified body! It was rampant in Europe in the Middle Ages and caused many deaths. When the Europeans went to the Americas, they carried the disease with them. Many more Aztecs in Mexico

That Dread Disease

and Native Americans were killed by smallpox than in the many battles with the Europeans. It was a disease that cut across social and economic class. During Jenner's time, it accounted for one in three deaths among children.

The smallpox virus is called variola and enters the body through the lungs. It is then carried by the blood to all the organs and finally spreads to the skin. The patient gets fever and headaches, and feels nauseous. After a few days, pink spots appear on the skin. These grow bigger and form blisters. They eventually fall off, leaving scars or pockmarks. In many cases, the patient gets blood poisoning and dies.

Many people had tried to find cures or preventive measures for this dreaded disease. One common method was immunization, the method of making the body produce resistance to a disease by using bacteria or viruses that have been modified or killed. There is evidence that around 600 BCE, the Chinese used to inhale smallpox material (such as the scabs and pus taken from someone suffering from the disease) through the nostrils. In eighteenth-century Bengal, there were specialists who would scratch people with smallpox material. There were also remedies arising out of superstitious beliefs.

A fairly common preventive measure during Jenner's time was variolation, a practice introduced in England from Turkey in 1721. Some skin and flesh was taken from someone with smallpox and scratched into the skin of another person who did not have the disease. This led to a mild case of smallpox, which was supposed to create immunity in the body, and prevent a major attack of the disease. However, since little was known about the disease, it frequently resulted in the death of the person it was supposed to protect. Jenner himself had been variolated when he was in school and he suffered so much that he never forgot the experience.

After Sarah's visit, Jenner decided to test the common lore

about the connection between cowpox and smallpox. He persuaded his gardener's eight-year-old son James Phipps to be his test patient. He made some scratches on James's arms and rubbed some material from Sarah's pocks into them. James became mildly ill with cowpox after a few days. This proved to Jenner that cowpox could be transmitted not only from cows to people but also from person to person.

This was merely the first stage in Jenner's experiment. The second and crucial stage was to check whether a person who had suffered cowpox was immune to smallpox. This involved exposing James to smallpox, a step which caused Jenner considerable disquiet. What if his theory was wrong and the poor boy lost his life?

On 1 July 1796, Jenner variolated James. To his great relief, James did not develop smallpox! After this, Jenner tested James several times with exposure to the smallpox virus but the boy was immune. James became the first person in human history to be vaccinated. The word 'vaccine' is derived from the Latin *vacca*, which means cow.

Jenner continued his intensive experimentation. In 1798, he finally published his work.

It would seem logical that a path-breaking technique which could protect people from a deadly disease would become immediately popular. But that was not to be. The surgeons who had made a lot of money variolating people were obviously opposed to this simple and safe cure for smallpox. The general public was also somewhat reluctant—many on religious grounds as they did not want their bodies to be contaminated by material from diseased cows.

Jenner spent a lot of time trying to convince his colleagues and the public about the effectiveness of vaccination. He was so totally involved in spreading the message of vaccination that he jokingly referred to himself as the 'vaccine clerk to the world'! Finally in 1853, Britain made vaccination compulsory for smallpox.

> Jenner was an enthusiastic and innovative gardener. He imported seeds from Europe and grew them in his garden. He was an expert in fruits like figs and raspberries. In 1818, he brought some grapevines from a famous vineyard and grew his own vineyard. Even now, almost two hundred years later, these produce fruit.

How does a vaccine work? Basically, a vaccine is something that is designed to protect the body against an infection.

Infections can be caused by many different kinds of living organisms. There is a wide variety of disease-causing organisms, and for each of these there is a different remedy. The most common disease-causing organisms are bacteria (which cause pneumonia and tuberculosis), viruses (smallpox, chickenpox and the common cold) and parasites (malaria, intestinal worms).

Our body is designed to fight most infections. As soon as the body senses the presence of a foreign body inside it, the immune system gets triggered. The body produces antibodies to fight the invader. If the antibodies win, you don't normally notice the disease-causing organism! But if the bacteria or virus wins, you fall sick and have to be treated with antibiotics and other medicines.

Given the vast number of diseases there are, how does the body know what kind of antibodies to produce? It so happens that the body remembers which foreign agents it has encountered and produces the appropriate antibodies for it. And it is this property that vaccines use to protect you against deadly diseases.

A vaccine usually contains either a dead, harmless or milder form of the infection that it will protect you against. In some cases, small microscopic parts of the deadly organisms are also used. When this vaccine enters your body, the body immediately reacts by producing antibodies to the foreign agent. It creates what is called an immune response. These antibodies are able to fight off the mild infection easily, and you don't even feel sick. But in the process, the body comes to know the infection and learns how to fight it. If you are ever actually infected with that disease, the body already knows which antibodies to produce and fight the infection. The immunity or defence of the body to the infection is lifelong. Once you have had chickenpox, for example, you will never have it again in your life because your body now has antibodies against it. Isn't it amazing? Can you even imagine a machine doing all these wonderful things which nature has ensured that our bodies do?

In the light of how vaccines work, it is possible to understand what happened to the Native Americans when they first met the Europeans. The American continent was separated by vast oceans from other continents, and there was no smallpox virus present. As a result, the Native Americans never developed any antibodies to smallpox. When the Europeans, who were either suffering from the disease or had been infected but were not actively ill, came into contact with them, they passed on the infection. Without the natural defences of the body to fight the infection, hundreds of thousands died a miserable death.

The cowpox virus, with which Jenner infected James and his other patients, produces the antibodies that are similar to the smallpox antibodies. Thus a person who has had cowpox would have the antibodies within him and that would make him immune to smallpox!

Once Jenner's vaccination had proved to be successful, there was continuous progress in developing vaccines for other deadly diseases. In 1885, Louis Pasteur, the French scientist about whom we will read more later, made the rabies vaccine. Plague, tuberculosis and tetanus are some of the other diseases that were conquered by vaccination. In 1955, an American scientist Jonas Salk developed a vaccine for polio, a deadly disease that used to leave many children paralysed for life. With mass vaccination in developed countries, polio became a thing of the past in many parts of the world. Sadly, in India, despite massive Pulse polio programmes, we still have not been able to eliminate this scourge.

Over time, most countries started vaccination programmes for children and were able to bring down the deaths and distress caused by childhood diseases like diphtheria, measles, mumps and rubella.

But what about smallpox? Jenner's vaccine was improved over time. Finally, a milder, inactivated form of the smallpox virus was used as a vaccine. And yet, despite the vaccinations, in the first half of the twentieth century, there were periodic epidemics of the deadly disease which left thousands dead and many more marked for life.

In 1967, the World Health Organization (WHO) started a campaign to get rid of this disease for good. At that time, there used to be around fifteen to twenty million cases of smallpox every year, mostly in Africa and the Indian subcontinent. To ensure that the world becomes smallpox free, it was essential to vaccinate every person in these regions. This was a mammoth task that involved a lot of money and many dedicated teams of health workers in many countries. But the prize was worth the effort. In a few years, the number of cases dropped dramatically, though there were still occasional cases.

The next stage of the programme was to isolate every single patient and make sure that he or she did not pass on the infection to others. All the people who had been in contact with the diseased person were vaccinated. The whole programme was almost like fighting a war!

The last reported case of smallpox in India was in 1975. In 1977, a hospital worker in Ethiopia contracted smallpox. He was immediately isolated so that the infection did not pass on to others. He was the last person on our planet to catch smallpox.

The WHO waited for another three years before declaring that smallpox has been eradicated on earth. Finally, modern science had been able to slay the deadly speckled monster! It is estimated that in the twentieth century alone, smallpox killed as many as 300 million people, making it the most deadly infectious disease.

> The last samples of smallpox virus are now kept in two laboratories in the US and in Siberia. In the unlikely case of a revival of the infection, these will be used for the manufacture of vaccines. The samples are protected like nuclear bombs because in the hands of wrong people, they could be much more devastating than nuclear warheads.

Jenner devoted his life to smallpox vaccination. He received many awards and prizes for his work. The story goes that during the Napoleonic wars, Jenner requested Napoleon to release some British prisoners. Napoleon is reported to have said, 'I can hardly refuse Jenner anything!' and obliged promptly.

> Jenner was an avid fossil hunter. Since childhood, he collected fossils from the banks of the river Severn near Berkeley. In 1819, he discovered the fossilized remains of the sea monster now known as plesiosaur.

In 1801, Jenner had predicted that his work would one day result in the annihilation of smallpox. It had taken humanity almost two centuries to achieve this. This one man's work has been responsible for saving more human lives than any other individual. The entire science of immunology—or the study of the body's defence against infection—can be thought of originating from Jenner's work.

Vaccines have saved hundreds of millions of human lives since Jenner's time. There are now vaccines for all major diseases though there are still some which remain unconquered. Malaria and AIDS are two notable examples of diseases for which effective vaccines have not yet been developed. But a new generation of combination vaccines is now available where a single shot immunizes one from several diseases.

The Smallest World

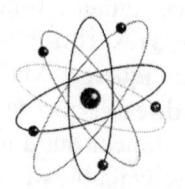

For his mother's birthday in 1792, John Dalton bought her a pair of blue stockings. On seeing his gift, his mother was horrified. 'Why have you brought me these red stockings?' she asked. Dalton was perplexed at this. He called his brother Jonathan to check the colour of the stockings. Jonathan confirmed that they were blue! Their mother, now also perplexed, summoned some of her friends from the neighbourhood. They all asserted that the stockings were indeed red. This was how, at the age of twenty-six, John Dalton discovered that both he and his brother were colour blind!

Today, Daltonism is the name given to colour blindness. But John Dalton did not change the world in terms of optometry or research into sight; what he shed light on was the story of the smallest constituent of all matter, the atom.

The story of atoms does not begin with John Dalton, but many centuries earlier. During the greatest years of the Greek civilization, philosophers like Aristotle, Plato and Socrates were active in trying to understand the world that they saw around them. For them, unlike for us, there was no distinction between different areas of knowledge. You didn't have biologists or chemists or mathematicians or sociologists—a learned man could write on all these and more. Aristotle, for example, wrote on politics, physics, biology, astronomy and literature!

A Greek philosopher called Democritus (460–370 BCE)

The Smallest World 57

thought a lot about what all the substances in the world were made of. If one took a piece of stone and broke it into two, one would get two pieces of stone. If one continued breaking the pieces over and over again, eventually what would one find? Democritus asked his teachers this question and found that no one had any satisfactory answers. Democritus realized that the process of dividing up of a piece of stone had to end somewhere—ultimately one must reach some substance or particle that cannot be further divided. He called this particle the atom, from the Greek *atomos*, meaning indivisible.

According to Democritus, all matter was made up of tiny, indivisible atoms. If one took a piece of some pure element, say iron, and kept on dividing it into smaller and smaller parts, one would ultimately get to a point where no further division was possible. This smallest bit of the iron is the atom of iron.

But is the atom of iron different from the atom of copper? Democritus thought that all atoms were made up of the same basic substance, but atoms of different elements had different sizes and shapes. What distinguished one element from another were the differences in size and shape, along with how the atoms arranged themselves. However, Democritus also believed that two different elements could have the same atoms. For the Greeks, if two elements had similar properties, their atoms were identical.

> For Democritus, diamond and graphite would have different elements—as a diamond is very hard and graphite is soft enough to be moulded into pencils. However, we know that they are both made of carbon, and therefore their atoms would be identical.

Democritus believed that atoms of water were so smooth that they could easily slide over each other, leading to the easy flow of water. On the other hand, atoms of iron were strongly attached to each other and hence iron was solid. The universe consisted of two things only—atoms and empty space. All substances were made up of these fundamental things.

As we have seen earlier, Greek philosophers like Aristotle based their theories about what we would now call scientific subjects on philosophical beliefs rather than on experimentation and observation of phenomenon around them. However, in this case, it was physically impossible to verify or refute Democritus's theory. There were no experimental tools available with which they could study atoms—such as spectrographs or atomic force microscopes we have today. In fact, the situation did not change for many centuries.

> Democritus is also known as the Laughing Philosopher because he proposed that happiness or cheerfulness was what all human beings must aim for as the highest condition.

This was pretty much the situation when John Dalton was born in 1766 in England. His father was a weaver, and his mother sold paper and ink to make ends meet. Dalton's parents belonged to a religious sect called Quakers. Quakers believe that a part of God exists in every human being and hence they try to live their lives according to Christian notions of truth, sincerity and simplicity. Dalton and his brother went to a Quaker school, where Dalton impressed his teachers with his mathematical ability and general intelligence.

At the age of twelve, when most of us are busy having a good time and going to school, Dalton took charge of a Quaker school! Many of the students were older than him, but he managed to control them without too much trouble. He returned home to his parents' farm after two years of this.

The Smallest World 59

In 1781, at the age of fifteen, Dalton and his brother took charge of a school in Kendall. The school had sixty students and Dalton frequently had to take on outside jobs to make ends meet. Nevertheless, he remained at the school for over twelve years.

It was during his time at Kendall that a wealthy Quaker merchant realized how intelligent Dalton was and decided to help him develop his skills. He started teaching Dalton mathematics and meteorology. More importantly, the merchant shared his excellent library with Dalton. Dalton's love for meteorology lasted all his life. He maintained a diary with 200,000 entries on the weather!

In 1793, Dalton moved to Manchester to teach in a college. In the same year, he published his first scientific work, *Meteorological Observations and Essays*. He developed an interest in chemistry, which he taught his students using a book written by the great French chemist Antoine Laurent Lavoisier.

> Lavoisier (1743–94) was a lawyer though his first love was chemistry. He experimented with several substances and made careful measurements to determine their composition. He also wrote the first modern book of chemistry, in which he listed the thirty-three elements we know of today. His work gave the science a modern footing and introduced the nomenclature (naming) system.
>
> During the French Revolution, Lavoisier was charged with plotting against the new regime and imprisoned in the infamous fortress of Bastille until he was guillotined. A contemporary French scientist wrote, 'It took but a moment to cut off that head, though a hundred years perhaps will be required to produce another like it.'

Inspired by the work of Lavoisier and other chemists, Dalton started experimenting to understand how two elements combined to give a substance whose properties were totally different from the constituents. For instance, water is a chemical compound of hydrogen and oxygen, and yet the properties of water are not the same as those of its two constituent elements.

In 1803, while trying to understand how various gases interacted, Dalton started thinking about atomic theory. Dalton found that oxygen and carbon can combine to make two compounds, carbon dioxide (the gas we breathe out) and carbon monoxide (a highly poisonous gas found in the exhaust fumes of cars).

Dalton discovered that each of these compounds had its own weight ratio of oxygen to carbon. Three units of carbon combined with four units of oxygen to give carbon monoxide while three units of carbon were needed for eight units of oxygen to make carbon dioxide. For the same amount of carbon, carbon dioxide had twice as much oxygen as carbon monoxide, or double the oxygen was needed to form a litre of carbon dioxide than needed to make a litre of carbon monoxide. As he increased the number of compounds he studied, Dalton found that elements combine with other elements in fixed ratios and occasionally in multiples of these ratios.

Dalton proposed his atomic theory in his book *A New System of Chemical Philosophy*, published in 1808. In this, he began from Democritus's idea that elements were made of tiny particles called atoms. Unlike Democritus, Dalton said that all atoms of an element were identical and had the same mass (or weight) but were different from atoms of other elements. Thus, all atoms of iron were absolutely the same but were different from atoms of all other elements. The properties of the atoms determined the properties of a substance.

Consider diamond and charcoal. Both are made of the element carbon. Yet, diamonds are hard while charcoal is soft. According to Democritus, diamond atoms cannot be the same as charcoal atoms. According to Dalton, the atoms of both are identical. The difference in their properties is due

The Smallest World 61

to the way the atoms are arranged.

The other important tenet of Dalton's atomic theory was that atoms of elements combined in fixed ratios to form particles of compounds. He did not identify these particles of compounds but these are what we today call molecules, the smallest unit of a compound that has its properties—much like atoms of pure elements.

> The exact date of Dalton's work on atomic theory is not known because his original papers were destroyed in the German bombing during World War II.

Dalton continued to work on many different projects while at the same time lecturing and propagating his ideas on atoms and chemistry. He discovered butylenes, compounds of carbon and hydrogen (hydrocarbons) which are used to make synthetic rubber, and also determined the composition of the compound ether that was used in medicine to make patients unconscious during surgery. He also developed a system of chemical symbols and arranged all the known elements into a table according to their atomic weights (the weight of their atoms relative to the atom of hydrogen).

Dalton was a recluse with few friends. He never married and dedicated his life to science. As befitted his Quaker faith, he was a man of simple habits and attire.

In 1822, Dalton became a fellow of the Royal Society, a very big honour for a scientist. He was awarded the Society's Gold Medal in 1826.

> When Dalton went to meet the king of England, he refused to wear the customary clothes. However, he agreed to wear his honorary robe from Oxford University. Being colour blind, he thought that the robe was grey in colour, when in fact it was red!

On 27 July 1844, Dalton took the measurements of the

weather and duly recorded them in his meteorological journal, a habit he had maintained for over fifty-seven years. Soon after this, he suffered a stroke and died.

The city of Manchester gave him a funeral fit for a king, for he was their most famous citizen. It was his wish that after his death, doctors carry out research on his body to determine the biological causes of colour blindness. For the great scientist, this was to be the final experiment!

The First Computer

Charles Babbage, a student of mathematics at Cambridge, was sitting in the library one day. The year was 1812, and the day was particularly cold and damp. As he worked on some calculations using logarithm tables, the warmth of the room made him very sleepy.

Babbage was almost asleep when a friend teasingly asked him what he was dreaming about. Babbage replied, 'I am dreaming that all these tables might be calculated by machinery one day.'

This must have provoked a lot of laughter in the library but was an astonishingly accurate prediction. And the person making it went on to conceive the first computer, which would do much more than calculate tables. The general principles that Babbage articulated are still used in modern-day computers.

Babbage was born either in December 1791 or January 1792. His father was a wealthy banker and his mother came from a wealthy landowning family. Despite his privileged childhood, he was a sickly child. He studied at various private schools and finally entered Cambridge University in 1810.

As a student of mathematics, Babbage had to work with logarithm tables to do calculations. The mathematician John Napier developed logarithms in 1614. Logarithms are basically tables of numbers that allow one to multiply and divide very large or very small numbers without too much effort. The only problem is that the accuracy of the result depends on the accuracy of the logarithm tables. And making accurate logarithm tables was a very tedious task in those days. It took a large number of people working for several years to be able to produce an accurate table. No wonder Babbage, as he worked, dreamt of a machine to calculate the complex figures.

After graduating, Babbage moved to London and worked on various mathematical topics. He got married in 1814 and was elected a Fellow of the Royal Society in 1816 at the young age of twenty-four.

Around 1819, Babbage got interested in astronomy. Possibly as a result of the long calculations involved in astronomy, which necessitated the use of logarithm tables, he went back to the idea of a machine that could automatically calculate the tables of logarithms more accurately than ever before.

> In the early 1800s, the French inventor Joseph Marie Jacquard created an automatic loom. The Jacquard loom could be used to weave very intricate designs on cloth. The basic idea behind this innovative device was to have a set of punched cards where the pattern to be woven can be stored. The threads on the weaver's loom pass through the series of punched paper cards and reproduce the pattern on the cloth. Even today, some of the most intricate and fine weaving is done using Jacquard's idea.
>
> Although it is not referred to as such, the Jacquard loom was possibly one of the earliest computers. It was a really clever idea, though the weavers of France did not think so. They hounded Jacquard out of the French city of Lyon because they thought that his invention would make them lose their livelihood. Emperor Napoleon, however, realized the importance of this invention and honoured Jacquard.

It was not that people had not thought of machines to do

The First Computer 65

calculations before. In 1623, a German scientist called Wilhelm Schikard had made a machine with interlocking wheels to perform calculations. In 1642, the famous French mathematician Blaise Pascal invented a machine that could add and subtract. Unfortunately, this machine, of which Pascal built about fifty, was used mainly in the drawing rooms of aristocrats as novelty items!

Babbage set out to create the machine of his dreams in 1819. By 1822 he had constructed a small model of the device that he called a Difference Engine. To actually build the machine required a lot of money and Babbage approached the government to finance the operation. The government paid him a sum of £1500, which was a lot of money at that time. He was told to complete the machine in three years. Thus began work on the most ambitious mathematical machine ever built.

Work on the machine proceeded very slowly, and the time period given to him expired. Expenses kept mounting. In 1827, Babbage's father, wife and two young children died. These tragedies took their toll on Babbage and he became ill himself.

> In 1827, Babbage published a book of logarithms from 1 to 108,000. He was appointed the Lucasian professor of mathematics at Cambridge, a post which Newton had held.

From 1828 onwards, the government was increasingly reluctant to give Babbage any more money. This went on for some more years when finally in 1834, the government refused to pay any more. They had already spent £17,000 on this project, and Babbage had spent about £6000 of his own money as well.

In 1833, Babbage met Ada Lovelace, the daughter of the great English poet Lord Byron. She was an accomplished mathematician, a versatile sportsperson and a talented musician. She had a fascination for all things mechanical and would spend hours taking apart mechanical devices and putting them together again. Meeting Babbage was a turning point in her life and she became an ardent fan of the mechanical mathematical devices that Babbage was thinking of and trying to construct.

It was around this time that Babbage made extensive drawings of another mechanical device, the Analytical Engine. Unlike the Difference Engine which was meant to calculate logarithmic tables only, the Analytical Engine could perform any calculation. In that sense, it was the first general-purpose computer to be designed. It never proceeded beyond the drawing stage because no one was willing to give Babbage money to build it despite his many efforts. The debacle with the Difference Engine was still fresh in people's minds.

In its conception and design, the Analytical Engine was remarkably similar to the modern-day computer. A modern-day computer is an amazingly versatile device. All computers, from the PC sitting on your desk to the huge machines used to predict the monsoons, have some basic things in common. These are outlined by Babbage in his drawings for his Analytical Engine.

What is it that makes a computer? Babbage described five components for his machine. These were the store, the mill, the control, the input and the output.

The store contains all the data that has to be calculated or processed as well as the result of the calculations. In this sense, the store is much like the RAM in your computer or even the hard disk drive that stores all the data and the files.

The mill is the central part of the machine that does all the calculations. It is the Central Processing Unit (CPU) of your computer, the chip that characterizes the computer. Most of today's machines have a Pentium IV CPU, working at a speed of 2.4 GHz.

The control is the set of instructions that will tell the machine what to do. The same machine could be used to perform different tasks depending on the control used. In today's computers, it is the software residing in your computer that tells it to, for instance, make your sports car in *Need For Speed* go fast or turn a corner. Your PC too can perform different functions, such as allow you to play *Need For Speed* as well as check your email.

The input and output for the machine perform functions like your keyboard (or mouse) and the monitor (or printer).

Of course, Babbage did not have microprocessors or RAM chips! But the logical construction of the machine is so similar to the modern-day computer that it can be called the first computer. Babbage's design used interlocking gear wheels of varying diameters, pulleys, chains and other such mechanical devices. For the control (software), Babbage used punched cards of the type that Jacquard had used in his loom. Thus, to perform any kind of operation, one had a set of punched cards which told the machine what to do. If one wanted to perform another calculation, one would need another set of cards, just as you need to install new software if you want your computer to perform new tasks.

> Babbage hated street musicians. In a book titled, *Observations of Street Nuisances*, he calculated that 25 per cent of his time had been destroyed by street nuisances including street musicians. This did not endear him to the street musicians. In fact, once a brass band played for five hours continuously outside his house!

Babbage had a wide range of other interests. He was fascinated by the newly introduced railways and is supposed to have developed the first cowcatcher that one sees in front of railway engines. He also played a major role in getting the broad gauge approved as the standard for the railways in Britain. The other work credited to him include things as diverse as the dynamometer, uniform postal rates, occulting lights for lighthouses, Greenwich time signals and the heliograph opthalmoscope.

Babbage was absolutely fascinated by numbers and statistics. In 1857, he published a note in a magazine titled, 'Table of the Relative Frequency of the Causes of Breaking of Plate Glass Windows'! In this, he made a meticulous study of 464 breakages of windows, of which 'drunken men, women, or boys' were responsible for fourteen! At other times, he got interested in keeping a daily account of the food eaten by zoo animals or in making tables on how much wood a person can cut in a day!

Babbage was fascinated by fire. He once baked himself in an oven at 130°C for about five minutes! He claimed to have not suffered any serious discomfort. He also lowered himself into Mount Vesuvius (the active volcano in Sicily) to see for himself how molten lava looked.

Lovelace worked with Babbage on the ideas for his Analytical Machine and wrote them down in great detail. However, she fell ill and died in 1851 at the age of thirty-six.

Years of fighting for funds for his Analytical Engine made Babbage a very bitter man. Despite his genius, he died virtually unknown in 1871. The unfinished parts of his Difference Engine gathered dust in the Trinity College.

Though unknown in their own times, the genius of Lovelace and Babbage was recognized later. A computer language developed by the Department of Defence in the US is named after Lovelace and a crater near the North Pole of the moon is named after Babbage.

> In 1908, Babbage's brain, which had been preserved in alcohol for thirty-seven years was dissected at the Royal Society by one Sir Victor Horsley who had to remind the Society that Babbage had been a 'profound thinker'.

A team of scientists, working at the British Museum, constructed the Difference Engine in 1991, in strict accordance with the detailed drawings left by Babbage. This machine works very well and calculates up to a precision of thirty-one digits! Babbage would have been a very pleased man had he been around to witness this feat. There are now plans to construct the Analytical Engine from his drawings though finding the money for it is proving to be difficult!

The Age of Electricity

One day, a customer came into George Riebau's bookshop in London to get a copy of the *Encyclopedia Britannica* rebound. Riebau had just hired a thirteen-year-old apprentice bookbinder and decided to give him a chance at binding the volume. The young boy, Michael Faraday, was thrilled. Though he had little formal schooling and could just about read and write, he had an unquenchable curiosity for knowledge. Faraday read the *Encyclopedia* and it was as if a whole new world had opened up before him! He copied the articles which he found interesting, especially those on electricity and chemistry. This impressed Riebau but little did he realize that his apprentice would one day be hailed as one of the greatest scientists of all times!

In the early nineteenth century, the scientific world was in a state of ferment. In the previous century, several scientists had studied a new phenomenon called electricity. The Italian scientist Volta had made a battery that gave a current when connected to a metal. He used copper and zinc plates separated by a chemical solution to get a current. The invention of the battery was crucial as a reliable source of current for other scientists who were getting to be very interested in this curious phenomenon.

> Volta's contributions to the science have made him a household name even today—just look at any electrical tower and you will see a small, red board with a skull and two bones, loudly proclaiming 'DANGER, 440 Volts'.

The Age of Electricity

Faraday was born in 1791 in a poor family. His father was a blacksmith who became ill by the time Michael was around five years old. The family was devout Christians and this religious upbringing influenced Faraday throughout his life. Faraday attended school for some time, but his family's poverty forced him to take an apprenticeship with Riebau in 1804. Soon he became a bookbinder, a job he did for the next nine years.

Though the work was hard, the advantage was that it allowed the poor boy to read many books that came to the shop to be bound, and to which he would have otherwise had no access. Faraday's education thus started by reading all sorts of books in the bookseller's shop!

The subjects which especially fascinated Faraday were chemistry and electricity. He started attending public lectures on these topics. Public lectures on topics of popular interest were a significant part of nineteenth-century life in London. These were held either at some savant's house or at public institutes, where eminent speakers in different fields would talk about their work to the lay audience.

In 1812, Faraday attended the lectures of the famous scientist Humphrey Davy at the Royal Institution in London. Impressed by the lectures, Faraday took detailed notes. He sent these notes to Davy with a letter asking for a chance to work with him. Davy advised him to continue working as a bookbinder and pursue science as a hobby since the chances of making a livelihood with science were small!

However, Davy's assistant left him and in 1813 Faraday joined him as an assistant. This was the big break which Faraday had been waiting for. Soon after this, Davy took him along on an eighteen-month scientific tour of various laboratories in Europe. It was during these months that Faraday learnt about the work that other scientists were doing in electricity.

After his return to London, Faraday worked mostly on chemistry for several years. He made some very important discoveries, including that of benzene that is used in many chemicals.

> Faraday liquefied chlorine in 1823. This had useful industrial applications in bleaching, making other chemicals and purifying water. The liquefied chlorine is much simpler to transport than the gas.

The Danish scientist, Hans Christian Oersted was conducting experiments with a battery in 1820 when he observed something very peculiar. Whenever a current passed through a wire, a compass needle placed close by behaved very strangely. Instead of pointing to the magnetic north, the needle would move whenever a current was passed close to it. Clearly, the electric current was producing a magnetic force that made the needle move. Oersted had discovered that there was a connection between electricity and magnetism! Others, like the French scientist Ampere, refined Oersted's conclusions by showing that two current-carrying wires would repel or attract each other if placed side by side.

After hearing about Oersted's demonstration of the production of magnetism from electricity, Faraday became obsessed with the idea of attempting the reverse. If electricity could generate magnetism, why not the opposite? He struggled with this question for the next ten years while continuing his work in chemistry.

In 1831, Faraday finally proved that magnetism could generate electricity. He showed that by moving a magnet near a conductor, say a metal wire, one could produce a current in the wire. This phenomenon, called electromagnetic induction, is what lies at the heart of the production of electrical energy. What Faraday had invented was the first electrical dynamo. With it, he effectively demonstrated that it was possible to

The Age of Electricity

convert mechanical energy into electrical energy. The mechanical energy could be from your muscles (in the case of a cycle dynamo) or from falling water (in a hydroelectric power plant) or even steam (as in a thermal power plant). But the crucial thing is that whenever there is a motion of a wire in a magnetic field, there is a current in the wire. The magnetic field could be a small one, as in a cycle dynamo, or very large as is found in the huge turbines running inside power plants which produce electricity for you and me.

Faraday started wondering whether a magnet could move a wire carrying current. That the current has an effect on the magnet had been shown by Oersted. But can one make the wire move because of a magnet? To see this, Faraday did what he did best, namely hook up a device to test it out! He connected one end of a wire to a battery and put the other one in a vessel of mercury. Mercury was a conductor of electricity and also allowed the wire to move freely. When a magnet was put in the mercury and the current allowed to flow in the wire, Faraday saw that the wire moved in a circle around the magnet! Faraday had just made the world's first electric motor, a device that makes possible so many of our modern-day appliances and machinery.

> Apart from inventing the electric motor and the dynamo, Faraday was responsible for working out the laws of electrolysis. This is the phenomenon which is nowadays used in electroplating metals with other metals.

With his hard work and intelligence, Faraday made up what he lacked in terms of schooling and education. He never got a degree from a university or college, yet he made discoveries which were monumental for science and technology. He was elected to the Royal Society in 1824 and, ironically enough, received an honorary degree from the University of Oxford in 1832!

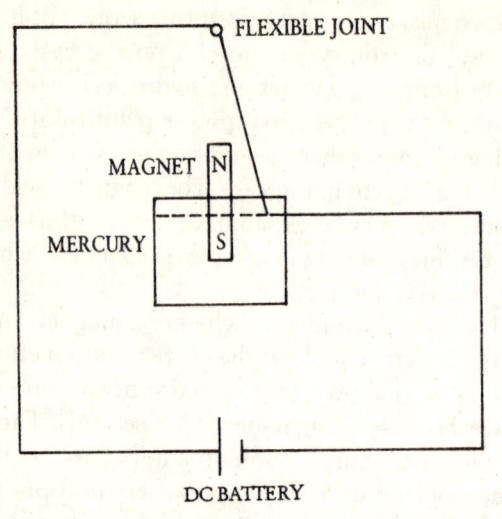

Faraday's Apparatus

In 1826, Faraday started a series of annual lectures for children at the Royal Institution that continue to this date. Now they are televised and attract a lot of viewers. Among the famous people who have delivered these lectures was the scientist Carl Sagan. Faraday himself gave a series of lectures called 'The Chemical History of the Candle' which were very popular and continue to be regarded as classics even today.

> When Faraday was asked by the British government to use his scientific knowledge to develop poison gases for use in the Crimean War, he firmly refused.

All the hard work started taking a toll on Faraday's health. He had a breakdown in 1839 but recovered fully in 1845 to continue his work. He worked on the electrical properties of materials as well as the effect of magnetism on light. When he died in 1867, he had established himself as the greatest scientist of his times.

The Age of Electricity

> When the prime minister of England visited Faraday's laboratory, he could not comprehend the importance of the dynamo. He asked Faraday what use the funny-looking machine had. Faraday is believed to have replied, 'I know not, but I wager that one day your government will tax it.'

Although Faraday was the first person to demonstrate the principles of the electrical dynamo and the electrical motor, he did not devote any time to improving the two devices. That was left to others, notably the famous American inventor Thomas Alva Edison and an eccentric Serbian inventor Nikola Tesla. Edison soon realized that the dynamo made by Faraday could be used to produce electricity on a large scale. He greatly improved the design of the dynamo and thought of a scheme to supply electric power to a city through wires. In the first demonstration of this, he hooked up his laboratory in Menlo Park and showed how electricity produced by his dynamo could be used to light the incandescent bulbs, once again developed by him! Later, Edison established an electric company and became enormously rich because of its profits.

Nikola Tesla came to the US from Budapest in 1884 and worked with Edison as his assistant. A year later, he set up his own laboratory. He was a brilliant inventor and developed the alternating current dynamo, a device that was different from the direct current dynamo developed by Edison. For a long time there was a bitter fight over which technology was better for electricity generation, and ultimately Tesla's dynamo was adopted the world over. The huge electric generators that produce the power that we use in our homes today are built on the principle that Tesla invented.

Unlike Edison, who was a very shrewd businessman as well as a scientific genius, Tesla never patented his inventions. As a result of this, he lived and died a poor man. Tesla worked in diverse areas, including radio transmission, much before

Marconi and others. He also thought of using radio waves for detecting enemy ships, a technology that was later used in radars.

By the beginning of the twentieth century, electricity was being used not only for street lighting but also more and more for manufacturing. As it happened, the person responsible for it, Faraday never profited from this.

Imagine our world without electricity and you will realize the importance of Faraday's inventions. His life is an example of what a person can do with hard work and determination, even when he does not have the benefit of any formal education.

The Age of Steel

In 1323 BCE, eighteen-year-old King Tutankhamen of Egypt died. He had been king for only nine years. He was given a grand traditional burial near the city of Luxor.

In 1922, two British archaeologists discovered his tomb. There was more gold in the tomb than the government of Egypt had in its bank at that time! But more importantly, Tut had with him a royal weapon—an iron dagger with a hilt made of gold and decorated with crystal. The dagger blade had not rusted in the three thousand years since Tut's death!

Iron was a truly valuable commodity in the time of King Tut. And iron and steel continue to be equally important in our own times. Imagine a world without cars, buildings, skyscrapers, machinery—everything that we associate with modern living is based on iron and steel.

Iron makes up around 5 per cent of the earth's crust. However, it does not occur in its metallic form but as a compound with carbon, oxygen, sulphur and other elements. Extracting the iron metal from its compounds is much harder than extracting copper from its ores. This is the reason why human beings used bronze (an alloy of copper and other elements) long before they used iron. Archaeologists have found bronze artifacts from around 4500 BCE while the first use of iron is from around 1600 BCE!

We now know a lot about the chemistry of iron and its ores but when it was first used, these were learnt purely from observation, trial and error. Possibly a clever Bronze Age smith, working with copper ore, discovered that along with the copper that he got from the furnace was a dense spongy mass of material. This spongy mass was the iron ore which had been mixed with the copper ore. The clever smith found that if he heated and hammered the spongy mass repeatedly, he could get a mass of metal that was very different from copper. This would have been what we now call wrought iron, a fairly pure form of iron metal. What the smith had done, without knowing, was to convert the iron ore into metallic iron.

When iron ore, which is often found as a compound of iron, carbon and oxygen known as siderite, is burnt with charcoal, it reduces to iron. But the trouble is that copper-making furnaces work at low temperatures because copper melts at a much lower temperature than iron. So, the iron formed would still be solid with the impurities from the ore still inside it. The repeated heating melts the impurities and hammering squeezes them out to leave pure iron that could be used to make weapons or precious trinkets for kings.

> This was not the only way to get iron. Our planet is constantly bombarded by meteorites, some of which carry iron. In the olden days, the iron in these meteorites was used to make weapons like King Tut's dagger. The Aztecs in Mexico also made the royal weapons from meteoritic iron. This iron was prized more than gold in most ancient civilizations.

The process of making wrought iron worked well with small quantities of iron. But it was very laborious and expensive, which explains why objects made of iron were rarely found in everyday use until about the fourteenth century. As time went on, the bellows and charcoal of the village or royal blacksmith gave way to blast furnaces which

The Age of Steel

used iron ore, coke and limestone. The iron obtained in this way usually contains impurities, such as phosphorous, copper, nickel and carbon. Carbon comes from the charcoal or coke that is used in the furnace while the others are present in the iron ore itself.

Ordinarily, impurities would make the metal useless. But one 'impurity' found in iron actually makes it into a wonderful substance—steel. Steel is a compound of iron and carbon (about 0.5 to 1.5 per cent). Steel is much harder and stronger than wrought iron. But if there is more than 2 per cent carbon in the iron, its properties change dramatically again. It melts at a lower temperature than wrought iron and is very strong but very brittle. This form of iron is known as cast or pig iron. Because it is relatively easy to melt, it can be easily cast into any shape.

Steel was known to our ancestors, who found that its hardness allowed for sharper edges in swords and weapons. As early as AD 200, Chinese blacksmiths were making steel. Over the centuries, the process of making steel took so much time and energy that the material was used almost exclusively for making sharper swords and royal daggers. Steel could become a mainstay for everyday life only when a brilliant Englishman transformed the way in which it was manufactured.

> Around AD 100 the Han dynasty in China used steel tools to crush the barbarian invaders from the north and south. In 1061 AD, the Chinese used more than fifty tons of cast iron to construct a thirteen-storeyed pagoda. The fourth-century, seven-metre-high iron pillar at the Qutub Minar in Delhi is a marvel of metallurgy that has withstood more than sixteen centuries of sun and rain and shows no sign of rust!

Henry Bessemer was born in 1813 in England in the family

of a rich engineer. As a boy, he was always interested in science and technical things, though he did not have much schooling. At the young age of seventeen, Bessemer fell in love but needed money to marry his beloved. To earn this money quickly, he started inventing things which were useful for daily life.

Bessemer's first commercially successful invention was embossed stamps. The title deeds for land and houses had to have a £5 stamp on it (this is like buying stamp paper nowadays for legal documents). These stamps could be peeled off, and so many people would avoid buying the stamp and just reuse the one from an old deed. The government was losing huge sums of money as a result of this. Bessemer invented a way to emboss stamps that could not be reused. As acknowledgement for this work, which earned the government a lot of revenue, he was offered the post of the Superintendent of Stamps.

> Bessemer was thrilled about the offer because he could use the money to get married. However, he told the stamps department about another invention where one could put dates on stamps. Perhaps daunted by his enthusiasm, the government decided that they did not need his services. Bessemer was very bitter and wrote many letters about how he had been 'rewarded' for his invention!

> Bessemer invented the process of compressing soft graphite (a form of carbon) into hard lead pencils, the kind we use today. He sold off his invention to a friend for a measly £200, and the friend made a lot of money!

Bessemer was a restless inventor and a shrewd businessman. Over the course of his life, he took out over a hundred patents that made him enormously wealthy. Among the other things invented by Bessemer was a hydraulic machine to extract sugar-cane juice, steam-driven ventilating fans for mines and a special furnace to make sheet glass.

> In 1840, when Bessemer's sister asked him to do a decorative title page for a portfolio of her paintings, he bought some bronze powder to use in the paint. This was very expensive and so he set himself the task of making it cheaply. He did not patent the process, but made a secret factory where only five people were allowed and hired his brother-in-law to run the plant. He managed to keep the process secret for over thirty years, making more money than he could have if he had patented the idea!

In 1854, Bessemer built a long projectile mortar to replace the heavy cannon balls that the army used. The elongated shape of the projectile would allow grooves to be cut on the surface. These grooves would make the mortar come out spinning. Making a projectile weapon spin gives it more accuracy in hitting the target, than a cannon ball which merely follows its trajectory (or path) according to the force of gravity and atmospheric friction. This trajectory is not very stable.

Bessemer took out a patent on the mortar. However, he found out that the new shells were heavier than the older cannon balls and the barrels of the existing cannons were not strong enough to use these. As steel was expensive and scarce, guns and other heavy artillery were made of wrought iron, which was nowhere near as strong as steel.

At that time, steel was made by heating bars of wrought iron with charcoal for several days. For each ton of steel, over 3 tons of coke was used, and the steel was sold for over £50 a ton.

In order to make money from his new mortar, Bessemer realized that he would have to find a way to make steel more cheaply so that cannons could be made from it. The story goes that he was ill and lying in bed when the idea of making the Bessemer converter came to him.

Bessemer was not the first person to think of a quick and economical way to make large quantities of steel. American William Kelly had created a similar process in the US but he never patented it. Bessemer modified and patented the process in 1855 and went on to make an enormous fortune out of it.

The basic idea in the Bessemer converter was to blow air into molten pig iron. Since pig iron contained a high concentration of carbon, the oxygen in the air reacted with the carbon to form carbon dioxide and carbon monoxide. Apart from oxidizing the carbon, the oxygen removed impurities like silicon and manganese.

The whole process was carried out in a huge oval steel container lined with clay or limestone. The container was pivoted on a huge stand, which could be tilted to remove the contents. This container was called the Bessemer converter and had a capacity of up to 30 tons. Iron was introduced into it from an opening at the top. At the bottom were numerous channels from which air at high pressure was pumped in. The process took about half an hour, after which molten steel was poured out from the top. The impurities either burnt away at the mouth or stayed behind as slag.

Bessemer did not succeed with his first design of the converter. There were several mishaps, explosions and other accidents. But finally when it worked, it was hugely successful. The Bessemer converter used very little coke and could be used to manufacture several tons of steel at one go. Steel could be produced for as little as £7 per ton!

This one invention changed the world. Cheap, plentiful steel made possible many machines, bridges, weapons and even cutlery that could not have been made with wrought iron. Bessemer started his own steel works and made an enormous amount of money not only by selling steel but also by allowing others to use his patented process.

The Age of Steel

> Not everything that Bessemer invented was successful. As he felt very seasick when he travelled to France on the English Channel, in 1869, he decided to build a boat in which the passengers would not be seasick. He spent a lot of his own money to design and build such a boat. Unfortunately, the boat was very difficult to steer and sank in the English Channel on its maiden voyage in 1875.

Bessemer was knighted in 1879 and also elected a Fellow of the Royal Society. When he died in 1898, he was a very wealthy man despite his failed adventures with a seasick-proof boat.

The process he had invented was to change life in the nineteenth century. With steel becoming as cheap and plentiful as wrought iron, many new things were made from steel. Different kinds of steel were also made by adding small quantities of metals like chromium or vanadium, which gave the steel new properties. For instance, adding chromium to steel makes stainless steel which is resistant to rust. Or adding molybdenum and chromium makes steel light and very strong, ideal for use in aircrafts.

Iron and steel have shaped human history in ways that few other materials have. Two accidents of nature have made this possible. The first is the enormous amounts of iron ore available on earth, and the second is the availability of vast quantities of coal to convert the iron ore into iron and steel. But for these two accidents of nature, the story of human civilization would have been very different.

The Descent of Man

On 27 December 1831, a ten-gun British ship left the south-western coast of England to commence a three-year voyage around the world. The object of the journey of the *HMS Beagle* was to survey the Pacific coast of South America and take precise measurements to help the British Navy with their navigation maps. The captain of the ship was a young man called Robert FitzRoy. Among the seventy-four members of the crew was the twenty-two-year-old Charles Darwin, who had just finished a degree from Cambridge University.

The voyage of the *Beagle*, which eventually took five years, proved to be as important for humanity as the earlier voyages of Vasco da Gama or Christopher Columbus. Darwin's work on this voyage led to an idea that has been called the single most important idea of all times, and which has revolutionized the way humankind regards itself.

Darwin was an unlikely addition to this expedition. His official position was that of a naturalist, to record the plants and animals that the ship would encounter during its voyage. But he was not trained to be one! The main reason for his inclusion on the voyage was because the captain wanted someone to talk to and eat with during the long journey. In those days, captains of ships did not mix socially with their crew who were usually from the poorer classes.

Darwin was born in 1809 to wealthy parents. His father was a doctor and his mother was the daughter of a very wealthy industrialist. Darwin's grandfather was the famous

The Descent of Man

eighteenth-century intellectual Erasmus Darwin. Darwin finished school in 1825 and was coaxed into studying medicine at the University of Edinburgh to follow in his father's footsteps. This was before the use of anesthesia and antiseptics became common. Surgery was a very messy, painful and bloody affair! A couple of visits to the operation theatre convinced Darwin that he could not bear the sight of blood and he abandoned his studies.

In 1827, Darwin enrolled with the University of Cambridge to become a clergyman. Here he met two people who were the biggest influences in his life. Adam Sedgwick, a geologist, and John Stevens Henslow, a naturalist, opened up new horizons for the young man. Darwin learnt a lot about the existing theories of the earth from Sedgwick and was trained to collect and store samples of flora and fauna by Henslow. Darwin's interest in natural history was fuelled by Henslow, who recommended him for the job on *Beagle*. Darwin's father was resistant to the idea but relented on the intervention of Darwin's uncle, Josiah Wedgwood II. And so it was that this half-trained enthusiast was accepted abroad the *Beagle* as an unpaid naturalist.

> For the first few weeks on the *HMS Beagle*, Darwin was so seasick that he only ate raisins.

After getting over the bouts of violent seasickness, Darwin got down to the business of observing, recording and collecting samples from all the places where the *Beagle* halted. The *Beagle* sailed along the Atlantic coast of South America, through the straits of Magellan, and up the Pacific coast of the continent. It then crossed the vast Pacific to Australia, onwards to Mauritius in the Indian Ocean, around the southern tip of Africa and finally back to England.

This was Darwin's first journey abroad, and he was

absolutely astonished to find the huge variety in the plant and animal kingdom in the places where the *Beagle* stopped. This led him to think about the history and variety of life on earth and the various ways in which this diversity of life could have arisen.

Darwin was not the first to think about these issues. Throughout human history, people have conjectured about the presence of the enormous variety in nature. All religions of course have their own theories regarding how life in all its diversity was created on earth. In Europe, most people adhered to what was stated in the Bible: that the earth was created some 6000 years ago and God created all the organisms on earth as they are now. It was impossible for people to even conceive of how any natural process could have created complex living beings like the humans!

The Biblical view of human history had already been challenged during the seventeenth and eighteenth centuries by scientists such as Copernicus, Galileo and Newton, who asserted that nature follows its own laws. Many people were aware of the debate about whether religion or science was the right tool to study the natural world. There was a growing interest in the question of how various organisms came to be on earth. Fossils had been found which did not support the Biblical theory of creation. To extrapolate from the Bible, the creatures we see today should be the same ones which went into Noah's Ark, and all fossils were relics of the Great Flood. However, the nature and age of fossils found contradict these beliefs. This was problematic for the Biblical theory.

There were also geological discoveries that made the earth certainly much older than 6000 years. At that time, it was believed in the scientific community that the earth was about twenty to thirty million years old.

Darwin was well aware of the controversies in geology.

Most scientists, such as the French anatomist Georges Cuvier, believed that the earth experienced successive phases of animal and plant life, each of which was destroyed by sudden catastrophes. The catastrophes wiped away all life and new forms came about after that. But once created, the species were unchanging till they were wiped out by the next catastrophe. This view was challenged by the English geologist Charles Lyell (1797–1875), among others, who believed that the changes on earth are not sudden but rather more gradual and operate over much longer periods of time.

Among the strange places that the *Beagle* took Darwin to was a group of islands called Galapagos in the Pacific, off the coast of Ecuador. Here he saw a variety of living and fossilized animal life that seemed to agree with Lyell's view of gradual change. But he also noticed something else. Each of the islands in the Galapagos had its own variety of tortoises, finches and other animals—similar in many respects and yet distinct species. It was this oddity that occupied Darwin when he came back from his voyage in 1836, complete with many trunk-loads of notes and samples of animals, plants and rocks.

Back in England, Darwin got down to recording his observations of the voyage, which was published as *The Voyage of the Beagle*, and continued to think about the issue of related but distinct species. By 1838, he had worked out the basics of his theory of evolution through natural selection. He spent the next twenty years refining and developing his idea.

Darwin married in 1839 and moved to an estate near London. He and his wife had ten children, of whom only seven survived to adulthood. Darwin, being a wealthy man, never had to work for a living and thus could devote all his time to his pet theory and other natural history projects like insectivorous plants and plant breeding. He also published several papers on geology.

In 1858, Darwin received a letter from Alfred Russell Wallace, who lived in the East Indies (present-day Indonesia). Wallace outlined his own ideas on how species evolved. Darwin was shocked to see that Wallace's ideas were almost identical to what he had been gradually developing for the last twenty years! This persuaded Darwin to finally publish his work.

> The Theory of Evolution was formally announced to the world on 1 July 1858 at a meeting of the Linnaean Society of London, whose role as outlined in their first charter of 1788 was 'the cultivation of the Science of Natural History in all its branches'. Darwin was not present at the meeting because he was at the funeral of his eighteen-month-old son who had died of scarlet fever.

In November 1859, *On the Origin of Species by Means of Natural Selection* was published and it was sold out the very first day! This book created a sensation almost immediately. Scientists, the clergy and even the man in the street read it as it proposed something so revolutionary that it was hard to ignore. It has been called one of the most influential books of all times.

The essence of what Darwin said was that evolution of life forms was a process of natural selection. All of life is a competitive struggle for natural resources. Imagine an animal living in a forest. It must eat and make sure that predators do not eat it. It must also ensure that it breeds so that the species continues.

Darwin proposed that within each population of any species, there are always some individuals who have certain characteristics that make them more likely to survive—it could be sharper beaks to get more food, or camouflage body to hide from the predators, or horns to fight off the predators. These individuals are obviously more likely to survive and hence reproduce. They pass on their characteristics to their offspring. Since this offspring is more likely to survive than the offspring of other members of the species who do not possess the favoured characteristics, over a period of time such individuals take over the whole population. This gradual process of natural selection thus produces a combination of features and adaptations that enable all life forms to make the best of their environment.

A peacock has gorgeous feathers so that he can attract the female members of his species to mate with him. Perhaps, in a distant past, all peacocks did not have equally colourful feathers. However, the ones with the best feathers would have the most chance of mating and reproducing, thus passing on this trait to the next generation. Over many generations, all the peacocks had colourful feathers. This is true of any trait.

Another tenet of Darwin's theory was that all organisms had evolved from a common ancestor. Different species branched off from this ancestor at different times and evolved into what we see today. Evolution is a slow and gradual process. What is more, it is a random process. The peacock does not think that it needs colourful feathers—it is just that some time in the distant past, there emerged peacocks with colourful feathers that had a better chance of surviving and reproducing. Over a long time, the peacocks that evolved all had this favourable characteristic.

These ideas met with immediate opposition. Most scientists were critical of Darwin because he did not articulate how these favourable traits were passed down generations. They also pointed out that the earth was far too young to support this theory. In the twenty to thirty million years, there had been just enough time to produce all the variety of life forms seen on earth. Furthermore, if Darwin was correct, there should be many more fossils of transitions between the species, the so-called Missing Links.

Darwin could not answer these objections. It was only in

the late nineteenth century that Gregor Mendel formulated his laws of genetics, which articulated how the mechanism for passing on the favourable traits between generations would work. It was the early 1900s before these laws were known to the scientific community. The question of the age of the earth was only settled in the early part of the twentieth century when it was established through radioactive dating that the earth was around four billion years old. The Missing Link problem could be ignored as fossils form only under very special conditions and it could be possible that the so-called Missing Links never formed fossils or we just haven't been able to locate them.

> Fossils form when the animal (or plant) dies and is preserved in sedimentary rock, such as shale, sandstone or limestone. Furthermore, the remains have to remain undisturbed over thousands of years so that the process of sedimentation can take place. Animals with soft tissue usually do not form fossils, and so most fossils are of skeletons, shells and wooded part of plants.

There were many other aspects of evolution that Darwin's theory could not explain. Not because these were not correct but because science had yet to find the tools with which to answer the questions. His theory in its essence is now universally accepted, with the loopholes being plugged by our knowledge of genetics and molecular biology.

The most vicious attacks on Darwin came from the clergy. The idea that we could have evolved from animals and hence there was nothing special about humankind was just not palatable. Christian theology sees the creation of man as the ultimate act of a divine creator. The idea that we emerged because of some random events in the distant past was against everything that the scriptures said and so it had to be wrong!

The Origin of Species, as the book came to be called,

remained controversial for a very long time. Even a century after its publication, it was still a matter of debate in religious circles. It was only in 1996 that Pope John Paul II acknowledged that 'new knowledge has led to the recognition of the theory of evolution as more than a hypothesis'.

In the meantime, Darwin wrote several other books, including *The Descent of Man*, where he articulated connections implicit in *The Origin of the Species*, such as humans evolved from apes. He also continued his scientific pursuits.

It is believed that Darwin had picked up some mysterious infection during his voyage on the *Beagle* and this caused him to suffer from intense fatigue and intestinal problems all his life. His work earned him many honours, including being made a Fellow of the Royal Society. He died in 1882 and was buried in Westminster Abbey, alongside other greats like Isaac Newton.

It is hard to think of a scientist who has had a bigger impact on human thought. If Copernicus pushed us to an insignificant corner of the universe, it was Darwin who told us that even on our earth, we are but just an accident of natural phenomena.

Calling Across the Miles

10 March 1876 began as another ordinary day in the untidy laboratory of Alexander Graham Bell at 5 Exeter Place, Boston. His assistant, Thomas Watson, had just finished making yet another model of a machine which Bell thought would transmit sound like the telegraph transmits signals. Both of them had been working hard at this project. They had tried out several devices, none of which were completely satisfactory. The device that they were testing now was also quite crude—made from a wooden stand, a cup of acid mixed with water, some copper wires and a funnel.

And then it happened! Bell said, 'Mr Watson, come here, I want you!' into the funnel and lo and behold, Watson heard the words in the next room! The first telephone call had been made and an invention, possibly the most valuable patented invention in history, had just been demonstrated.

The invention of the telephone, a device that was going to change the way we live, is a complicated story. It has all the elements of a sensational film—suspense, intrigue and luck. And though the rewards and the fame that came with the invention went to Bell, it was an achievement shared by several inventors, many of whom are not well known.

The word telephone comes from the Greek words *tele*, meaning from far, and *phone*, meaning voice. People have always wanted to communicate with others far away. Early hunters probably communicated with their kin by building a fire in the jungle or building jungle drums or tom-toms, as

Calling Across the Miles 93

seen in the *Phantom* comics! Later, people used mirrors, flags or carrier pigeons to send messages.

For a start, a device that uses electricity to transmit sound, as the telephone does, could not have been even imagined before the advent of electricity—not even by the great visionary Leonardo da Vinci, who could imagine airplanes and helicopters! There was just no example in the natural world of the wonderful things that a telephone could do.

Bell was born in Scotland in 1847. His father was an educator who had developed a visible speech system to help deaf people speak. His mother was a musician and his grandfather a speech therapist. Thus acoustics, or the science of sound, was an integral part of Bell's upbringing.

After school and university in Edinburgh and London, Bell moved to Canada in 1870 and then to the US in 1871. He started teaching his father's visible speech system to deaf-mutes in Boston. In 1872, he set up a school to train teachers in the method. But this was just his livelihood.

His passion was developing a way to send messages across distances. The idea of a telephone had not yet occurred to him; at that point he was fascinated by the idea of a musical telegraph. With this device he thought he would be able to send several messages at the same time over the telegraph wires.

Telegraphy had already changed the way human beings interacted. It became possible, for the first time in human history, to instantly get news from distances that would have taken the fastest horses several weeks to cover. The inventor of this revolutionary device was a man named Samuel Morse.

Morse, the son of a clergyman, was born in 1791 in Massachusetts. While at university, he developed a passion for painting. After learning painting in Europe, he returned to the US in 1815. He began painting portraits in New York to earn his livelihood.

Like Bell later, Morse was also fascinated by the idea of long-distance communication. The work of scientists like Faraday had increased our understanding of electrical and magnetic effects so that it was possible for people to think of using them in other areas of life. In 1832, Morse thought about using them in communication and, in 1835, he built a working telegraph.

But building a working telegraph and convincing businessmen and politicians that it was a worthwhile invention were two different things. Morse tried very hard to raise money for building a telegraph network in the US, but no one seemed to be interested. He tried to arouse public interest. One of his biggest stunts was to lay a telegraph cable across the harbour in New York to demonstrate the utility of his invention. Unfortunately, on the day when he was to carry out this demonstration, the cables got stuck in a ship's anchor, and the sailors aboard the ship promptly cut the cable.

Morse refused to be embarrassed and persisted in his efforts. Finally, in 1844, he got some money to build a line from Washington to Baltimore. On 24 May, he transmitted the words, 'What hath God wrought' across this wire from Baltimore and it was received instantly in Washington. This demonstration was enough to convince the politicians that the telegraph was a useful thing for the country.

Soon, a large network of telegraph lines crisscrossed the country. News from the world of business, sports and politics could be transmitted instantly across the continent. The Pony Express and other forms of transcontinental communication soon became obsolete.

Morse also developed a code made up of dots and dashes to be used in telegraphy. His code was adopted all across the world, except for US and Canada, in the 1850s. It has slipped into disuse commercially with the advent of satellite communication.

Calling Across the Miles

> In 1866, the first transatlantic cable was laid and the Old and the New World became connected almost three and half centuries after Columbus had landed in the Americas.

Bell was very interested in inventing a device that would allow several telegraphic messages to travel simultaneously on the same wire. He managed to raise money for such a device from several wealthy patrons who were interested because telegraphy had become a very lucrative business.

While working on the musical telegraph, Bell got the idea of transmitting speech instead of just words as in a telegraph. His background in acoustics, together with all that he had learnt about electricity, convinced him that he was on the right track. But making a working model for such a device proved to be very hard. Bell laboured on for a couple of years, trying out various unsuccessful models.

In the meantime, he decided to apply for a patent for the telephone even though he did not have the device ready. A change in the rules of the Patent Office in 1870 meant that one no longer needed to have a working model to register a patent. On 14 February 1876, Bell filed for a patent for his telephone. And this is where the story gets intriguing!

It turned out that Bell filed his patent application just a few hours before another inventor, Elisha Gray, filed his application. There were rumours that Bell knew about Gray's work and thus wanted to beat him to it. It was also said that a key idea in the working of a telephone was not included in Bell's original application but only added later after Bell was shown Gray's application! There is still a lot of mystery as to what exactly happened on that crucial day. But whatever it was, it led to a lot of court cases and bitterness later on.

How exactly did the telephone work? The basic idea in a telephone is to convert the sound signals from your voice into electrical signals, send them across wires to another telephone where they are faithfully converted back into sound signals. And how does one convert sound into electrical signals? This was done by using the idea of a variable resistance.

Think of a simple electrical circuit, say a 1.5 V battery (pencil cell) connected to a small bulb of the kind one uses in a torchlight. The battery is basically a source of electric current that flows once there is a complete circuit for it to flow. One can think of the battery as a source of electricity just like your overhead tank is a source of water. The higher the voltage of the battery is, the greater the flow of electrons or current.

But the current is also dependent on a property of the circuit called resistance. Resistance, as the word suggests, is the capacity of the circuit to withstand the flow of current. Copper wires have low resistance while rubber has a high resistance. This is the reason that copper wires are used to carry electricity while rubber slippers protect you from getting a shock. For the same battery, a higher-resistance electric bulb will cause a smaller current to flow. This is just like having thinner water pipes that cause a slower water flow.

The amount of current in a circuit depends on the resistance of the circuit. This fact had been known much before Bell, but what Bell did was to use this together with the fact that sound energy can be used to move things. Taking a funnel which would concentrate sound because of its shape, he used it to move a very thin plate of metal called a diaphragm. As our voice hits the diaphragm, it moves in and out. This diaphragm is connected to a mechanism whose resistance increases or decreases with the motion of the diaphragm. Bell used a rod (connected to the diaphragm) that was dipped in a very weak acid. This, however, was very inconvenient and a box containing carbon granules soon replaced it. As our voice hits the diaphragm, it moves and so changes the resistance of the carbon granules. This means that the current in the electrical circuit changes. This is the conversion of sound into electrical signals.

What about those receiving these signals? The electrical signal now goes into the earpiece of your friend's telephone through wires connecting the two telephones. Here the magic of magnetism comes into play. In 1820, Oersted had demonstrated that electricity produces magnetism. If we wrap electrical wires around a piece of iron and pass a current, the iron becomes magnetic. The larger the current, the larger the magnetic field produced by the magnet. This effect stays for as long as the current is flowing. Such a magnet is called an electromagnet and is used in many household devices like doorbells and tape recorders.

The earpiece of the telephone contains an electromagnet and a diaphragm. The electric signal varies in intensity. This causes the magnetic field to change, which in turn makes the diaphragm move in and out. This motion of the diaphragm produces sound which we can hear.

Thus, Bell assembled all the pieces needed for a successful telephone: a mouthpiece that produced a variable current in response to your voice, wires that cause the current to flow along the wires, and an earpiece which could receive and convert the electric waves into sound.

Of course, this is only a simple model of a telephone that connects you to just one other telephone. In real life, there are a lot of electronic circuits in the telephone exchange which allow you to call anywhere in the world. And fancy electronic instruments that use quartz crystals, and not carbon granules and diaphragms, are what you probably see now in your house. But the basic idea of transmitting speech remains the same as in the time of Bell.

Throughout 1876, Bell and Watson worked to improve the telephone. They managed to increase the range and make the sound quality better. But this was still not enough for people to become interested in it as a necessity—it was treated like a curiosity.

> When you dial your friend's number, how is it that the phone rings in his house and not somewhere else? The part of the telephone network that works as a super-brain which sorts out where your call should go is the exchange. In the exchange, there are devices called switches that connect the signals from one phone to another. The switches are complicated and expensive machines, which are of various types, like the primitive cross-bar exchanges (still used in some of our smaller towns), analog switches and the most recent digital switches. The switches basically act as policemen who control and channel the traffic into its proper path.
>
> When you dial the desired number, your phone sends an electric signal to your exchange that routes the signal to your friend's phone. In the olden days, almost all telephone signals travelled through single copper wire pairs (of the kind you sometimes see next to railway tracks). With the tremendous growth in the number of phones, these proved to be inadequate and were replaced by coaxial cables. These are the thick, black cables that you see the telephone department laying when it has dug up all the major roads in your city! These are basically twenty to twenty-five wires running together and are laid underground. Glass fibres, made of a special kind of glass, carry light signals which are converted into electrical signals using special devices. These fibres can carry thousands of phone conversations and are much more reliable than copper wires. Microwave communication links are also used (these are the tall red-and-white towers near post offices) while satellites are used for long-distance communication.

In the meantime, other inventors developed their own designs despite Bell's patent. One such inventor was Thomas Edison, who developed a carbon mouthpiece. Ringers, exchanges and other innovations came slowly.

In 1877, Bell formed a company—Bell Telephone—with his wealthy patrons. They set up the first telephone line between Boston and Somerville, Massachusetts. This company, which was renamed AT&T, soon had most of the telephone business, making Bell a very wealthy man.

> On 21 February 1878, the world's first telephone directory came out. It was a single sheet of paper with fifty names!
> Also in 1878, the first telephone was installed in the White House. President R.B. Hayes made the first call to Bell who was sitting thirteen miles away. The president's first words to Bell were to speak more slowly!

Bell now had the money and leisure to indulge in his other pet projects. He co-founded the National Geographic Society and invented other things like an audiometer (to test hearing) and a very crude device for recording music. He got very interested in aeronautics and spent most of his time and money on making machines capable of flying.

> Bell applied the principles of aeronautics to boat design and in 1917 developed a hydrodrome, a hydrofoil boat. The boat reached speeds of about 115 kilometre per hour and was for many years the fastest boat in the world.

On 17 June 1914, AT&T raised the last telephone pole of the phone line that connected San Francisco to New York, and thus the first transcontinental phone line was complete. By the time Bell died in 1922, his invention to send voice across distances had truly revolutionized the world.

The Age of the Automobile

In the early 1850s, a young salesman was travelling to many small towns in western Germany, selling tea, sugar and kitchenware. We don't know how he was travelling—possibly horse-drawn carriages for short distances and trains for long distances—and it is not really relevant to our story, except for the fact that he was going to change the way all of us travel today. This was Nikolaus August Otto's third job after dropping out of high school at the age of sixteen. He had been a bright student, but Germany's economic crisis meant that his mother thought he would do better as a merchant.

During Otto's travels, he heard about the invention of a new kerosene-powered engine by a Frenchman, Etienne Lenoir, who had used it to drive a carriage. This engine was unlike anything that had been used before—it was an internal combustion engine. Otto got fascinated by the engine and, during his long journeys, thought about how it could be improved. In his long letters home to his girlfriend Anna Gossi, whom he had met at a carnival some years earlier, he discussed these ideas.

> When the fuel is burnt inside the engine, it is an internal combustion engine. Steam engines burn their fuel outside and hence are not internal combustion engines. The steam generated outside causes the piston to move in Watt's engine. In 1680, the Dutch scientist Christian Huygens designed, but never built, the first internal combustion engine. This was powered by gunpowder.

The Age of the Automobile

The nineteenth century had seen revolutionary advances in the field of transportation. Animals were replaced by trains drawn by steam engines and locomotives (first designed by George Stephenson in 1829), which transformed the movement of men and materials.

In 1769, a French Army captain, Nicholas-Joseph Cugnot, had built a three-wheeled steam-powered vehicle which can be called the first automobile. This vehicle could carry four people and a load of artillery. It had a speed of about three kilometres per hour but had to stop every fifteen minutes to build up steam in its external combustion engine. Several attempts were made to build lighter and faster steam-powered vehicles for individual transportation, but these were not very successful.

It was in 1860 that Lenoir invented a one-cylinder engine that used kerosene as fuel. Unlike the steam engine, the fuel burnt inside a chamber and provided the energy needed to push the piston. In 1862, a vehicle fitted with the Lenoir engine reached a maximum speed of about six kilometres per hour!

Nikolaus Otto, the son of a village postmaster, was born in 1832 in a small village on the Rhine river in Germany. His father died when Otto was still a child. Otto was a bright student, interested in mechanical contraptions, but was forced to drop out of school for financial reasons.

Otto was convinced that the Lenoir engine, though a great advance over previous engines, could be improved. Although it was popular initially as a replacement for steam engines, it soon fell out of favour because the engine was neither efficient nor practical. But for putting his ideas into practice, Otto needed finances.

> In 1861, Otto tried to patent a carburetor to improve the efficiency of the Lenoir engine but failed!

1864 was a lucky year for Otto. He met a businessman, Eugen Langen, and formed a partnership that proved to be crucial to the future of automobiles. Langen had an interest in designing machinery and was looking for new ideas. Otto's ideas for improvements to the Lenoir engine appealed to him and he immediately saw a lot of business potential. With Langen's money and Otto's expertise, they formed a company to improve the Lenoir engine and manufacture them.

After three years of hard labour, the company made a much-improved engine. This engine was very different from the original Lenoir engine and was vastly more efficient in terms of fuel consumption. Unlike the Lenoir engine, it was not noisy. There were two main problems with the Lenoir engine. The first was that it got heated quickly and had to be cooled down or it would seize. Cooling it required many gallons of water. The second drawback was that Lenoir used a gaseous fuel that needed to be stored and transported. Otto's engine, on the other hand, used liquid gasoline which was then mixed with air in a carburetor (which he had designed). This use of an air-fuel mixture made storage of fuel easier and also increased the efficiency. The Otto engine also did not suffer from the problem of overheating. There were other technical improvements which contributed to the new engine being vastly more efficient and quieter than the Lenoir engine.

The new engine quickly became very popular. A new company called Gasmotoren-Frabrik Deutz AG was formed in Deutz, near Cologne, to manufacture it. The engine was a runaway success—the factories at Deutz were working overtime and yet could not produce enough engines to meet the demand!

> Gasmotoren-Frabrik Deutz AG still exists today as Klockner-Humbolt-Deutz AG, the world's largest manufacturer of air-cooled diesel engines.

The Age of the Automobile

Among the people working in the factory was a young engineer, who had been trained as a gunsmith. Gottleib Daimler had years of experience in factories across Europe and was a fantastic engineer. When he came to work for Otto, Daimler brought along his protégé, Wilhelm Maybach, who would go on to become one of the greatest engine designers. It was the combination of Otto, Daimler and Maybach that proved crucial in developing automobiles.

In 1876, Otto built the four-stroke engine which revolutionized transportation for all times to come. This engine was the ancestor of the car engines in use today. Though there have been major improvements in the last century and half, the basic design is still the same.

> A four-stroke engine is what we use nowadays in automobiles. Many motorcycles and scooters till recently used a two-stroke engine. A two-stroke engine produces more power than a four-stroke engine of comparable size, but it is less fuel-efficient and leaves a lot more fuel unburnt. Hence, there is more pollution. Now all two-wheelers have four-stoke engines as well.

What is the four-stroke engine and what makes it so different? The underlying idea of an engine is to convert the hidden chemical energy in a fuel into motion. The chemical energy could be stored in coal or diesel or petrol or even hydrogen, as in the latest fuel-cell-driven vehicles!

The heart of any internal combustion engine is a metal cylinder with a movable piston. The cylinder has an inlet pipe and an exhaust pipe, both fitted with valves. The piston is attached to a crankshaft, a device that converts the up-and-down motion of the piston to the rotary motion needed to move the wheels in the car. The engine operation can be understood if we see what goes on at each stroke of the engine.

In the first or the intake stroke, the piston starts at the

top of the cylinder. The intake valve opens and, simultaneously, the piston moves down. A mixture of air and petrol is let in through the intake valve. Petrol and air are mixed in a separate device called a carburetor that is outside the engine. (This is just underneath the big air filter that you see when you open the bonnet of your car. The air filter cleans the air of dust and other particles while the carburetor mixes the air and the petrol.)

> Only a tiny drop of petrol is needed for each cycle of four stokes in the operation of the engine. The amount of chemical energy stored inside a drop of petrol is huge! One drop is enough to propel a small stone about 500 feet into the air!

The next stroke is known as the compression stroke. The piston is in its lowest position and the cylinder filled with a fine mixture of air and petrol. The inlet valve closes and the piston moves up, compressing the air-petrol mixture.

In the combustion stroke, when the piston reaches the top, the spark plug ignites the fuel mixture. This causes a huge explosion and the expanding gases push the piston. The energy from the fuel is thus being used to move the piston down.

Finally, the piston moves up again in the exhaust stroke. The exhaust valve opens and as the piston moves up, the exhaust gases are expelled out of the exhaust pipe at the back of your car. The engine is now ready to start a second cycle of intake, compression, combustion and exhaust strokes.

The up-and-down motion of the piston is converted through a crankshaft into a rotary motion which moves the gears in the gearbox. The gearbox is basically something that controls how much power from the engine is transferred to the wheels. When you start your car, you need more power than when you are cruising on the highway. Among other

The Age of the Automobile

things, the amount of friction between the tyres and the road is more when the tyres have to start moving than when they are already moving.

Of course, modern cars have a lot more than just an engine. The fuel pump is needed to pump the fuel from the fuel tank into the carburetor. The electrical system runs the spark plugs, lights and indicators. The cooling system cools the engine because otherwise it will melt from the heat produced in the cylinders. A suspension system makes your ride less bumpy, and a transmission system transmits the power of the engine to the wheels. But the heart of the car is still the internal combustion engine that powers it.

What we have described above is a one-cylinder four-stroke engine. Modern cars have more than one cylinder for more power and smooth driving. They also have more than two valves per cylinder and a fuel-injection system (instead of a carburetor) for better fuel efficiency.

> So now you know what it means for your car to be a four-cylinder, sixteen-valve 1000 c.c. machine! The 1000 c.c. refers to the total volume of the cylinder—the larger this volume, the more the fuel mixture it can hold and the more power it can produce per cycle. The Maruti 800 is only 796 c.c. while the powerful Skoda Octavia engine is 2000 c.c.

Although Otto had invented the four-stroke engine, he was not very interested in car manufacture. The engines sold by Otto were used primarily in small industries to replace the steam engines in use till then.

In 1882, Daimler and Maybach left Otto and started their own company to make automobiles! In 1885, they mounted an engine on a bicycle to make the world's first motorcycle. The following year, Karl Benz, another German engineer, built the first car—a three-wheeled vehicle with a four-stroke engine and a chassis forming a single unit. In 1889, Daimler and Maybach put one of Otto's four-stroke engines on a horse carriage. Several improvements to the basic design had been made in these years including better valves and more cylinders. In 1890, Daimler and Maybach started a car-manufacturing company called Daimler Motor Company. In 1925, this company merged with Benz's company to form Daimler Benz, the makers of Mercedes Benz cars today!

The automobile quickly caught the imagination of people around the world. In 1894, car manufacturing started in France. The first Peugeot automobile drove alongside the bicyclists in 1891 in the Tour de France, the 1046-kilometre bicycle race between Paris and Brest. The Fiat car company started making cars in Italy in 1899, as did several manufacturers in the US.

In 1894, a French company Panhard-Levassor began making cars with Daimler's patents. They introduced the clutch and gears for the first time in an automobile. They were also the first to introduce engines in front of the car—all cars before this had engines below the passenger seats.

One person in the US whose imagination was fired by the new vehicle was an engineer at the Edison Electric Company called Henry Ford. Ford quickly realized that the coming century would be the century of the automobile. He set up the Ford Motor Company in 1903 and started making cars numbered according to the English alphabet! The first, Ford Model A, debuted in 1903 while the famous Model T was introduced in 1908. Model T was a huge success and the company sold more than 15 million cars of that model until they discontinued production in 1927. The key to Ford's success was the introduction of the assembly line for manufacturing cars, an innovation that made cars cheaper

The Age of the Automobile

and easier to make. By 1920, more than 8 million Americans had cars. The automobile revolution was finally here.

But the one man responsible for this revolution could not witness this excitement. Nikolaus Otto died in 1891 in Cologne. By the time of his death, he was a rich man, thanks to his royalties and patents. Though the internal combustion engine has undergone much improvement since his times, his name is immortalized in the basic process used. The four-stroke cycle he invented for his engine is called the Otto cycle and is used to power almost all cars, boats and motorcycles today.

Let There Be Light

One day in 1879, the famous inventor Thomas Alva Edison was sitting in his laboratory in Menlo Park, New Jersey, absently fingering some carbon. He had been working very hard for the last few years to find a suitable material for use in an electric bulb—something that would not only produce light but also last a while before it burnt out. The trouble was that all the materials that he and his many associates had tried would burn out in a few hours. A few months ago, Edison had made a platinum filament bulb that worked well but burnt out fast. What he needed was something that would burn very slowly. Suddenly, Edison glanced down at the material in his hand. What if he started carbonizing various materials to use as filaments?

Edison was a very stubborn person. Once he got this idea, he and his associates immediately set about carbonizing filaments of every plant that they could get hold of. Edison also got botanists to send him filaments of tropical trees so that he could test them. In all, they tested about 6000 vegetable fibres but none seemed to work properly.

Finally, Edison tried using carbonized cotton thread as a filament in his electric bulb. The bulb glowed in a faint orange–yellow glow which lasted for over fifteen hours before burning out. This was all the encouragement that Edison needed. He and his associates started experimenting with changing the design and composition of the bulb. Finally, by the end of 1880, they produced a bulb that lasted for

Let There Be Light

over 1500 hours. The era of the electric bulb was finally here—human beings would no longer be dependent on candles, animal fat or gas lamps to light up their homes and workplaces.

Edison was possibly the world's best-known inventor, who invented some 1093 things that we know of. Born in 1847, he attended school for only three months. His mother read him most of the great classics, apart from teaching him elementary arithmetic and writing. At the age of twelve, he started selling newspapers on the Detroit–Port Huron section of the Canadian Grand Trunk Railway, which ran from Ontario through Toronto and Montreal, and crossed the border to Chicago and Detroit. He had an attack of scarlet fever that left him partially deaf—a disability which would be helpful in his later life when he wanted to concentrate on his experiments!

From an early age, Edison was very interested in mechanical and electric things. At the age of fifteen, he bought a second-hand printing press and started printing and selling his own newspaper on the Grand Trunk Railway! Since he spent most of his time on the train, he modified one of the freight cars into his laboratory, and tinkered there in his spare time. This arrangement worked well for some time, till one day the train gave a sudden jerk. Some chemicals were spilt and the freight car blew up!

A grateful stationmaster, whose child Edison had saved from being crushed under a train, taught him telegraphy. Telegraphy had already revolutionized communications and was used extensively in the railways. It was while working as a telegraph operator that Edison made his first invention—one that allowed a telegraphic message to be transmitted automatically over the second line even if the operator was not present.

> In 1868, at the age of twenty-one, Edison got his first patent—for a telegraphic vote-recording machine.

Edison moved to Boston from Port Huron, and started spending all his spare time doing research. He made a stock-ticker machine that would print the quotations from the stock market and this was a big hit. By selling this improved stock-ticker machine he earned $40,000. With this money, he established his own laboratory at Menlo Park, New Jersey, in 1876. This was the first laboratory in the world dedicated to industrial research.

The next ten years that Edison spent at Menlo Park were among his most productive years. First to come out of his Menlo Park laboratory was an improved telephone transmitter. Bell had demonstrated the use of telephone in 1876 but the first telephones could not operate over distances more than a few kilometres. Edison improved on the available transmitter and made it possible to communicate over hundreds of kilometres.

Next came what was probably Edison's most original idea—the electric phonograph. During his work on the telephone, Edison thought of using the sound energy to move a sharp needle which could cut grooves on a piece of waxed paper. This waxed paper could later be played and would generate the same sounds. The idea was an extremely original one and the genius of Edison was required to convert it into a device that worked. In 1878, he got the patent on the phonograph, though the development of the actual device happened a few years later.

Though the phonograph might have been Edison's crowning achievement (and Edison was justifiably very proud of it), the invention that possibly had the most impact on ordinary people was the electric bulb. After getting the patent on the phonograph, Edison started on the problem of the electric bulb in 1878.

The first person to use electricity for lighting was Sir Humphrey Davy. In 1811, this famous English scientist had demonstrated that an electric arc passing between two poles of a battery produced light. Thus was born the electric arc lamp which was not very practical. With many improvements in design, electric arc lights came to be used in public places in Paris and London. But their expense and size rendered them difficult to use in households. Several inventors worked on the problem of making a more efficient and easy-to-use electric lamp to replace the gaslights that were commonly used on streets and houses.

One such inventor was Sir Joseph William Swan. Swan found that the solution lay in not passing an electric current in air to produce light but instead passing it through a filament. Some years earlier, another Englishman, James Joule, had shown that the passage of electricity through any substance led to the production of heat. We see this happening in our electric kettle or our hot water geyser. Current passes through a metallic element that heats up. This in turn heats the water around it for your tea or your bath. Now if the current is made to pass through some suitable metal, the heat produced could be used to heat the metal to such an extent that it glows and gives off light.

Swan used carbon filaments to produce light. The problem was not yet solved though. What was needed was not just passing an electric current through a filament but also making sure that the filament lasted for some time and did not burn. This required an environment without any oxygen or air, since oxygen is needed to burn anything. The solution was to put the filament in a sealed glass bulb that contained no air. The glass would allow the light from the filament to pass through but would not let any air in to burn the filament.

This was the theory on which many people worked. However, putting it into practice was a not an easy task at all. Making a glass bulb which is strong enough to maintain a vacuum inside and yet thin enough for it to be transparent was a challenging task. More challenging though was to find the right material for the filament. The filament had to be able to withstand high temperatures needed for glowing without fusing or melting. Though Swan's bulb was not very long-lasting, he patented the use of the carbon filament in England in 1878.

This was when Edison turned to the problem. Edison had the advantage of not only having a large number of associates who could help him try out various ideas, but also his own glass-blowing facility. Swan's idea had been published in the journal, *Scientific American*. It is possible Edison read of it there. What cannot be denied is that he made vast improvements to what Swan had envisaged. The bulb Edison created was the first that lasted a long time, used a small amount of current, and gave off a moderate amount of light.

> Interestingly, among the thousands of materials tested by Edison in his laboratory was tungsten, which is commonly used nowadays in light bulbs. But the tools needed to work with this metal were not available then and Edison rejected it as unsuitable!

In 1879, Edison applied for a patent for the use of carbon filament in the electric bulb. Swan immediately took him to court, claiming that he had got the patent earlier. The courts in Britain ruled against Edison and forced him to take Swan as a partner in his business venture in England. (One could say that Edison's work was a carbon copy of Swan's!) In 1883, the US Patent Office also ruled that Edison's patents were invalid because they were based on earlier work. This

Let There Be Light

meant that Edison could no longer hope to make any money from his invention!

Nevertheless, Edison realized that an electric bulb without electricity is just a glass receptacle! So the shrewd businessman that he was, he set up an electric company which would supply electricity to households and businesses. Here, once again, he had competition from the eccentric Serbian inventor Tesla, who had developed a different way of producing and distributing electricity. Edison lost out on this one too because, over a period of time, Tesla's idea was accepted as more practical.

After his wife's death in 1884, Edison reduced his visits to Menlo Park. Instead, he set up a new laboratory in Glenmont, New Jersey, and lived there for the rest of his life. It was here, in 1890, that he developed the motion picture camera on whose design our modern-day movie cameras are based. He even established Edison studios in 1893 to produce movies! Many one-minute movies were made in this studio, including the first 'western'.

> In 1900, Edison started working on producing a reliable and portable electric battery. After eight years and a million dollars, he produced an alkaline battery with nickel. His design is still used in safety lamps for miners and aircraft runway beacons.

When Edison got started on his experiments, nothing could distract him. He would live in his laboratory, eating there, and sleeping just four hours a day. When a crucial experiment was in progress, he would not leave his laboratory for several days! Getting an original idea was one thing but making it work practically required a lot of hard work. And that was one quality Edison possessed in abundance. Just like he tried thousands of materials for the filament of the bulb, when, at the age of eighty, he started his investigations into making synthetic rubber he tested over 17,000 plants over a period of four years. He could find rubber in only about 1200 of them. As he said, 'Genius is one per cent inspiration and ninety-nine per cent perspiration'!

Honours and awards came to Edison from all parts of the world. The legendary American industrialist, Henry Ford, established a museum that housed a collection of Edison's many inventions.

The incandescent bulb that Edison had created underwent further improvements. In 1903, Willis Whitney patented a treatment for the filament so that it would not darken the inside wall of the bulb when it glowed. And in 1910, William Coolidge invented the tungsten filament that lasted much longer than Edison's filament. Since then, there have been other improvements to the structure of the bulb, such as using a coiled filament and filling the bulb with inert gases.

Edison died in 1931. The US government considered putting off the lights in the whole country for a minute as a mark of respect for him. This idea was considered to be impractical since electricity had become so important in everyday life by then!

Edison's many inventions had dramatically changed the world in the twentieth century. But the one invention that could be said to have had the most impact was the long-lasting incandescent bulb. With the work of Edison and others before him, human beings finally had a cheap and durable way to get rid of darkness.

The Invisible Enemy

On 4 July 1885, nine-year-old Joseph Meister was bitten by a rabid dog. Over the next day, the pain increased so much that he could barely walk. On 6 July, his mother decided to take him to see the famous French scientist Louis Pasteur.

The sight of the child in extreme pain moved Pasteur deeply. He instantly decided that he would take a gamble and see if he could cure the child. Though Pasteur had been carrying out experiments for curing rabies for several years, all his experiments had been on dogs. Experimenting with a nine-year-old child was a courageous step, especially since there was a chance that Pasteur's cure could lead to the boy's death.

Rabies is an acute infection caused by a virus that enters the body through the bite of an animal. The virus is found in most mammals, but is most prevalent in dogs, cats, foxes and bats. Once the virus enters the body, it affects the nervous system and has very bizarre symptoms. The patient finds it hard to breathe and is extremely thirsty. And yet, when given water, he or she cannot drink it. This symptom gave rise to the original name of the disease—hydrophobia, which is Greek for fear of water. After a few days, the patient almost always died.

Pasteur had experimented with the saliva of infected animals and soon concluded that the disease-spreading organism resides in the nervous system of the body. He then injected an extract from the spine of a rabid dog into a healthy animal and found that the healthy animal soon developed symptoms of rabies. After experimenting for several years, he was finally able to produce a much weakened form of the rabies virus which could be used for vaccination.

Pasteur had tested his vaccine on animals but now, to save the young boy from agony, decided to experiment with the rabies treatment. Miraculously, in a few days, the boy recovered fully. Joseph had been saved literally from the jaws of death.

Born in 1822, Pasteur grew up in the small town of Arbois. As a schoolboy, Pasteur was not considered particularly brilliant and his favourite pastime was fishing! However, his headmaster realized the boy's potential and encouraged him to go to Paris to study. But Pasteur, having grown up in a small town, was very homesick in Paris and had to be brought back by his father.

Pasteur did finally go back to Paris to earn his doctorate in chemistry from the prestigious École Normale in 1847. After this, he taught at universities in Dijon, Strasbourg and Lille. The University of Lille, which Pasteur joined in 1854, was in the main wine-producing region of France. The teachers in the chemistry department were frequently asked to help the winemakers with technical problems.

At this time, a major problem faced by the winemakers was the souring of their wines. Wine is made from the juice of grapes that contains fructose, a kind of sugar. When yeast is added to this and the mixture kept for some time, the sugar turns into alcohol, a process known as fermentation. But occasionally, the wine would taste sour, causing huge financial losses for the winemakers. Pasteur was approached to solve this problem.

Pasteur immediately realized that the production of alcohol is due to the yeast while the souring is due to micro-organisms.

The Invisible Enemy

These micro-organisms produce acids like acetic acid (vinegar) that resulted in the sour taste.

Knowing the cause was not good enough—what was needed was a solution. Pasteur suggested heating the grape juice to a high temperature to kill the micro-organisms and then fermenting it.

> Pasteur subsequently studied a similar process in milk and suggested heating the milk to about 65°C and then storing it hygienically. This process, which is used to this day, is called pasteurization. The next time you drink a glass of milk, think of how Pasteur made it possible for you to have fresh milk without falling sick. Today, the milk given by cows hundreds of miles from your city can be safely transported to you. Before Pasteur, the only way milk could be stored was to turn it into curd or butter.

This work saved the French wine industry and made Pasteur very famous. He was offered the prestigious post of director at the École Normale in Paris in 1857.

In 1865, disaster struck the world-famous French silk industry. A disease known as pebrine attacked the silkworms. The infected worms would die before making the cocoons. This was causing major losses and the government requested Pasteur to help the silkworm farmers.

Through his microscope, Pasteur saw that the diseased silkworms contained tiny organisms. By testing some uninfected worms, he was able to establish that the infection was spread by eating mulberry leaves that had the remains of the infected worms. He worked with the silkworm farmers to keep the silkworms in hygienic conditions and kill all the infected worms and the mulberry trees. Once again, Pasteur was able to save the livelihood of thousands of people.

Pasteur's work on the souring of the wine and the silkworm disease made him a strong believer in the close relationship between germs and disease. At this time, there were a lot of different theories regarding the origins of germs as well as their spread from person to person. It was widely believed that the microscopic germs spontaneously originate in whatever substance they are found in. Thus, according to this theory, the germs that Pasteur saw under the microscope in the wine or in the infected silkworms were born in the substance.

Pasteur had several fierce debates with the other scientists who were in favour of the theory of spontaneous generation of germs. Pasteur believed that germs were always introduced from the environment. Thus, the germs in the grape juice that led to it becoming sour were from the air or infected containers. Similarly, the germs that cause disease in us enter our bodies from the outside. This simple concept, called the germ theory of disease, may now seem like commonsense to you, but in Pasteur's time most doctors did not accept it. One of their arguments against this was that as germs were so small as to be invisible to the naked eye, they could not possibly kill much larger creatures like human beings and other animals!

Pasteur worked very hard at trying to convince his fellow scientists and doctors about germ theory and the need for better hygiene. He published a book called *The Germ Theory and its Application to Medicine and Surgery*, in which he asked doctors to clean their instruments, wash their hands and use clean bandages on wounds.

One person who heard about Pasteur's work was a surgeon in Edinburgh, Joseph Lister. In his experience of treating patients, Lister had observed that whenever there was an open wound, the flesh around it would start to decay. Lister was convinced that the micro-organisms Pasteur had talked about in his germ theory were causing the decay of the flesh. To test his theory, Lister covered his patients' wounds with cloth soaked in carbolic acid. Carbolic acid is the chemical that is nowadays used in hospitals (and gives hospitals their peculiar 'hospital' smell). To his surprise, Lister found that none of the patients whose wounds were covered got any infection.

Lister experimented some more and finally published his results in 1867. Initially, he met with a lot of resistance from his colleagues but soon the results were evident for everyone as the use of carbolic acid saved thousands of lives. Lister thus discovered antiseptics by using Pasteur's idea of the germ theory of disease.

> Every time you have a fall and your mother puts a little Dettol on it, remember it was less than 150 years ago that this simple method of saving millions of lives was discovered.

Pasteur worked on many other projects, including finding a cure for anthrax. Anthrax is a disease that is fatal for cattle and thus used to cause a lot of economic loss to the meat and dairy industry. Pasteur, on the request of the French government, studied the infected cattle and sheep but could not understand how the anthrax germ, which had been isolated and studied by another scientist Robert Koch, was transmitted from one sheep to another. He wandered around grazing grounds and farms till he found his answer. It turned out that the anthrax-infected sheep were killed and buried in land where there were earthworms. These earthworms fed on the carcasses and brought the spores of the germs above ground. When the healthy sheep grazed on this land, they ingested the spores and got infected!

> During the course of his research on anthrax, Pasteur noticed that chickens never caught anthrax. He guessed that this is because chickens have a body temperature of 43–44° C. To check this, he lowered the body temperature of a chicken to 37° C and found that it caught anthrax when exposed to the germs.

Pasteur was aware of the dramatic results achieved by the English doctor Jenner in controlling smallpox through vaccination. He prepared a vaccine for anthrax with weakened spores of anthrax. When injected into healthy sheep, this helped them develop immunity to the disease. Pasteur also worked on finding the causes and the vaccines for many diseases like cholera and diphtheria. It was during these studies that he started work on the rabies vaccine that saved the life of Joseph Meister.

After demonstrating the effectiveness of the rabies vaccine, Pasteur set up an institute in Paris for rabies. He continued to be its director till his death in 1895. The institute was named the Pasteur Institute after his death and continues to be the premier institute for research in microbiology and vaccines.

Long before his death, Pasteur had become a national hero in France. He was given a state funeral in the Cathedral of Notre Dame in Paris and his body was put in a tomb in the Pasteur Institute.

> Joseph Meister, the boy who first received the rabies vaccine, eventually became the gatekeeper at the Pasteur Institute. When the Nazis occupied Paris in 1940, they wanted Pasteur's tomb to be opened up. Meister refused and killed himself rather than be forced to desecrate Pasteur's tomb.

Pasteur was undoubtedly one of the greatest scientists of modern times, whose work not only increased our knowledge of disease but also resulted in saving the lives of millions of people.

Ruling the Airwaves

Just before midnight on 14 April 1912, the luxury liner *Titanic* hit an iceberg about 150 kilometres from the coast of Newfoundland, Canada. The ship was carrying about 2200 people on its maiden voyage. Built at a cost of about $10 million, the *Titanic* was considered to be unsinkable as it had all the latest technology. What followed after the collision was complete mayhem. There were not enough lifeboats for all the passengers and so the women and the children were sent off on the lifeboats while the men and the crew braved the icy waters. As this drama was unfolding, the ship's radio operator had sent desperate messages for rescue. Fortunately, another ship, the *Carpathia* was close by. It had received the radio message from another ship that had picked up the SOS from the *Titanic*. As a result, *Carpathia* was able to save about 650 people from the *Titanic*. And all this made possible by the wonderful invention of radio communication by an Italian, Guglielmo Marconi. It is a strange quirk of fate that Marconi and his wife were supposed to be on board the doomed ship that day. They had cancelled their trip at the last moment because one of their children was unwell!

It was only fifteen years earlier that Marconi had demonstrated the use of the radio or wireless for communication between ships and shore. Before the invention of the radio, once the ship had left the shore, there was no way to communicate with it till it docked at a port. The telegraph and the telephone, the other means of long-distance communication used on land, were useless on open seas. Marconi's invention of the radio made possible other things that we tend to take for granted today—cell phone, radar, cordless phones, radio-controlled toys and GPS receivers.

The radio was only the latest in the long list of devices and methods used by human beings to communicate over a distance. Though telephone and telegraph had already bridged huge distances, these still required setting up of an extensive and expensive wiring and equipment network. Radio changed all that—now even the remotest hamlet or village could be connected without waiting for the wires to reach it. While telephone and telegraph were limited by terrain, radio wasn't. And like most such inventions and discoveries, Marconi only happened to be the person to round off a process that had started with the German scientist Heinrich Hertz.

In 1888, Hertz was working as a professor of physics in Germany when he produced the first radio waves. His apparatus was crude, but it showed clearly that a new form of radiation was being generated. For a long time, these waves were called Hertzian waves.

> Any transmission of energy through space is called radiation. It could be sound radiation, which is a mechanical radiation because it requires the presence of a material medium, or electromagnetic radiation, like light and radio waves which do not need a material medium and can travel through empty space.

Hertz's work immediately sparked off a flurry of activity among scientists the world over. It was soon realized that the waves generated by Hertz were in reality electromagnetic waves, just like light and x-rays, except that these rays were much longer than either. While the wavelength of visible light is only around fifty millionths of a centimetre, radio waves can be as long as a few hundred metres.

Ruling the Airwaves 123

Among the many people who were working on radio waves was a bright young professor of physics at the Presidency College, Calcutta. J.C. Bose had joined the college after finishing his studies at Cambridge and London. He was interested in Hertz's work and during 1884–90 worked hard to develop a radio transmitter and a receiver. He generated and studied very short radio waves that were around 5 millimetres. He demonstrated their various properties like reflection and refraction, and even developed the first semiconductor.

> Semiconductors are materials which have made the fancy world of electronics possible. Normal materials that we encounter are either conductors of electricity, like metals, or insulators, like rubber and wood. Semiconductors are materials which have electrical properties that are sort of in-between conductors and insulators. These properties make them ideal for use in electronic circuits.

But Bose was not interested in the applications of his discovery—he was a scientist who was only keen on abstract knowledge rather than putting it to commercial use. For almost a century, people forgot about the fact that Bose had been the first person to develop the radio. Only recently has it been established that Bose indeed had worked on the radio much before Marconi.

> In 1865, at a public demonstration in Calcutta, Bose showed how radio waves could be used to ring a bell and even to explode gunpowder. In 1869, he transmitted radio signals for over a mile, and this was reported in the British newspaper the *Daily Chronicle*.

Though Bose studied radio waves before Marconi, it was left to Marconi to realize the immense potential of this new form of communication. Marconi was born in 1874 in Italy. He was the son of a wealthy Italian landowner and an Irish mother, who belonged to the family that distilled the famous Jameson's whisky. Marconi had a privileged upbringing. He went to school in Italy and England, and was also educated at home by private tutors. As a child, Marconi was interested in mechanical things and he would frequently devise scientific toys for his own amusement.

After school, Marconi tried unsuccessfully to join the Italian Naval Academy. His mother encouraged him to pursue his scientific interests, and so he went to study at the University of Bologna. A physics professor there introduced Marconi to the recently discovered Hertzian waves.

This immediately captured Marconi's imagination. He set to work to make his own radio. Working in his attic, he was able to send a signal across the room. By 1895, Marconi had succeeded in sending a signal a couple of kilometres across fields. By this point, he was convinced that he was on to something with a lot of commercial potential.

Marconi tried to get the Italian post and telegraph department interested in his invention, but they were unresponsive. Disappointed, he moved to England in 1896. As it turned out, while Marconi was experimenting in his attic, a British scientist at Oxford University had already succeeded in sending signals over 150 metres. But Oliver Lodge, like Bose, was only interested in the scientific aspects of the problem and hence did not bother to patent his system.

In England, Marconi filed an application for a patent on wireless telegraphy in 1896. At the end of 1896, he gave a public demonstration of his system at London and became an instant celebrity in London society. In early 1897, he was awarded the patent and formed the Marconi Wireless Telegraph Company in London. By 1898, Marconi was already experimenting with communicating with ships at sea. He transmitted the first message across the English Channel to France in 1899.

Ruling the Airwaves

> The eccentric Serbian inventor, Nikola Tesla took Marconi to court claiming that he had priority on the patent. The dispute was finally settled in 1943 when a US court ruled in Tesla's favour.

All these developments were well received by the governments of Italy, France and England. But the big challenge was to be able to get across the Atlantic. In 1900, Marconi took out his famous patent no. 7777 for 'tuned telegraphy'. In 1901, after spending an enormous sum of £50,000 on experimenting and designing the equipment needed for transatlantic communication, Marconi undertook what most people believed was an impossible gamble as the curvature of the earth would not allow such communication. He travelled to Newfoundland to test this equipment. After several accidents due to bad weather, on 12 December 1901, Marconi finally received a series of three dots—the Morse code for the letter S—across the Atlantic from the station in England.

> The first transatlantic signal was received by Marconi using a 400-feet-high, kite-supported antenna.

The era of the wireless had truly begun now! Telegraphy was now possible without the expense of laying down thousands of miles of cable.

> The first public radio broadcast took place from Massachusetts, US, on Christmas Eve, 1906. The broadcast included a verse from the Bible, a violin recital and a song!

But what exactly goes on in wireless communication? Actually, it is very simple to generate radio waves. Yes, you too can do it easily. Take a 9-V battery (the ones which are shaped like matchboxes) and an iron nail. Switch on your radio and make sure that it is not tuned to any station. You will hear some noise on the radio. Now go close to the radio and quickly tap the iron nail between the two terminals of the battery. What you will hear on the radio now will be a crackle caused by the radio waves produced by you! You could actually use this simple set-up to transmit a message using Morse code if you want.

What happens here is that the making and breaking of the electrical circuit (by the tapping of the nail) produces very weak radio waves. The same thing happens when a motorcycle starts near your house and you hear a crackle in your radio. The sparking in the spark plugs in the motorcycle produce radio waves that are received by the radio! In fact, the original production of radio waves by Hertz and others was by a sparking coil, very similar to what is used in the automobile spark plugs.

We have already seen, while discussing Faraday's work, that an electric current in a wire creates a magnetic field around it. What is even more surprising is that whenever there is a changing electric current in a wire, there is a current produced in a wire placed close by. This current only exists when there is a change in the current in the first wire. In the process of connecting and disconnecting the battery with the nail, you are changing the current in the circuit and producing electromagnetic waves.

Any system of radio communication consists of basically two parts—a transmitter and a receiver of the waves. As we have seen, a simple radio transmitter is your battery and an iron nail. Of course, the radio transmitters used for communication or in radio stations are much more sophisticated. But the basic principle is the same—we need to create a rapidly changing electric current in a wire. All the fancy electronics in the radio transmitting stations do just this.

We have already seen that we can use our simple radio transmitter to transmit dots and dashes. But what about the wonderful Kishore Kumar song that one hears on the radio? To transmit voice we need to do something much more. This process is called modulation. Modulation, as the term suggests, is basically the encoding of any useful information on to a radio wave. There are two principal kinds of modulations used in radio—amplitude modulation or AM (this is what we used to have before the advent of FM radio) and frequency modulation or FM.

Once you have produced the radio waves, you need a receiver to receive them. A receiver in its simplest form consists of an antenna (to receive the radio waves) and a device which will demodulate the radio wave to extract the information carried by it. The simplest demodulator is a diode, a device that is used in many electronic devices which allows current to flow only in one direction.

There are many other components to a radio that allow us to listen to our favourite radio stations. Every radio has a tuner, an electrical circuit that makes the receiver sensitive to only one wavelength. Thus, tuning your radio to 194 metres will make it catch only the radio station transmitting on that wavelength. Another essential component of the radio is an amplifier, which as the name suggests, enhances the weak signal received by the radio receiver. Apart from this, there will be other electronic components to improve the quality of sound and remove distortion and noise.

In 1909, Marconi received the Nobel Prize in physics together with Karl F. Braun, his competitor and one of the founders of a German radio company Telefunken. By now Marconi's fame had spread the world over. He received many honours and prizes for his work.

In 1935, Marconi gave the first practical demonstration of the radar. Radar, which uses radio waves reflected from objects to detect them, played a crucial role in World War II.

Marconi continued to work on improving short-wave radio communication. These are radio waves that can travel long distances because they are reflected from the atmosphere. He died in Rome in 1937.

> On Marconi's death, all the world's radio stations fell silent for a short time as a mark of respect. The airwaves became as silent as they had been before him.

In 1909, two ships *Florida* and *Republic* collided at sea in the North Atlantic and, had it not been for the wireless messages flashed by the ships' wireless operators, all 1500 lives would have been lost. After the disastrous sinking of the *Titanic*, the British postmaster-general commented that those who had been saved in the disaster had been saved because of one man, Marconi, and his wonderful invention.

Seeing Within

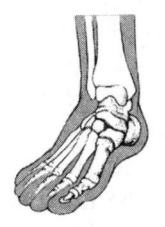

On 22 December 1895 Wilhelm Conrad Roentgen excitedly made his wife Anna Bertha come down from their top-floor flat to his laboratory in the basement of the Physics Department building where they lived, in Wurzburg, Germany. The excited professor of physics wanted to show her the fascinating thing he had discovered some weeks earlier. He asked Bertha to remain motionless for some time and flipped a switch. After a while, he showed Bertha the image of her hand. Except that this photograph of her hand was most unusual—there was a faint shadow of the flesh while the bones in her hands were clearly visible! The wedding ring on her finger was also clearly seen in the image.

Bertha's first reaction was fear. She was convinced that it was somehow a bad omen and she was going to die soon! Little did she realize that she was now part of the history of medicine as the first person whose body was x-rayed. Her husband had discovered something that would prove to be of immense value to humanity—not only in medicine but also in industry and scientific research.

About six weeks earlier, on 8 November, Roentgen had been working in his laboratory using a fairly common piece of apparatus called the Crooke's tube (now better known as the cathode ray tube found in your television or computer monitor). He had been studying for a while the various properties of cathode rays that were produced by the tube. On that day, he had enclosed the tube in a cardboard box, and when he put on the current, he was surprised to see that an object placed some distance away from the tube glowed in the darkened room! He found that the object was a photographic plate. This intrigued him greatly. How could the cathode rays have travelled through the cardboard and hit the photographic plate to produce a glow?

Over the next few days, Roentgen performed several experiments with the newly discovered rays. He found that the rays could easily penetrate many objects, including the human flesh. He did not share his findings with anyone. All he told a friend was, 'I have discovered something interesting, but I do not know whether or not my observations are correct.'

During those weeks, Roentgen was grumpy and preoccupied. He sat silently at the dinner table or took his meals down in his laboratory. By the time he brought Bertha down to see the magic, he was convinced that he had discovered something unusual. Since he did not know the nature of the rays, he called them x-rays, a name that has stuck for over a century!

On 28 December 1895, Roentgen submitted a paper to a German scientific journal in which he described his findings. Word soon spread in the university and the city that the shy professor of physics had discovered a way of seeing through things!

In January 1896, Roentgen gave the first public demonstration of his new apparatus and made an x-ray of a colleague's hand. His colleagues at the university wanted him to name the new rays after himself, but Roentgen was too modest.

Born in 1845, Roentgen was the only child of a cloth manufacturer. When he was three, his family moved to the Netherlands where he went to a boarding school. He showed no great talent in his school, and displayed enthusiasm only for wandering around and exploring nature. His love for nature stayed with him all his life and even when he was famous, his favourite pastime was trekking in the mountains. In 1862, he entered a technical school at Utrecht but had to leave soon. What happened was that some other student had made a cartoon of a teacher for which Roentgen was blamed. As a result of this, Roentgen was expelled.

He went to the University of Utrecht in 1865 to study physics because he had not got the qualifications to study engineering due to his expulsion. But he really wanted to become an engineer and for this he joined a polytechnic at Zurich, Switzerland, to study mechanical engineering. In 1869, he finished his PhD from the University of Zurich and after teaching at various places, joined the University of Wurzburg in 1888 as the professor of physics. In 1900, he moved to the University of Munich, where he remained for the rest of his life.

The new form of radiation that Roentgen discovered was subsequently investigated by other scientists. It was found to be just like ordinary visible light—only with a much higher energy or frequency. Visible light, x-rays and radio waves are all different kinds of electromagnetic waves. All of them travel at the speed of light, a huge 300,000 kilometres per second. What makes them all different from each other is their frequency or wavelength. Radio waves have a very large wavelength (the distance between the successive crests of the wave). Visible light is much shorter, and has a wavelength of around 50 millionths of a centimetre. X-rays are even shorter. Typical x-rays are around hundredth of a millionth of a centimetre. There are even shorter electromagnetic waves which you may have heard of—gamma rays produced in nuclear reactions and used for destroying tumours in cancer patients.

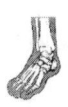

> One of the properties of electromagnetic waves is that the shorter the wavelength, the more energetic the waves are. Thus, radio waves are not that energetic while x-rays and gamma rays carry a lot of energy. This is why even though our bodies are constantly being bombarded by radio waves from radio stations and cell phone towers, we don't feel any ill effects while any long exposure to x-rays and gamma rays can be very dangerous.

How did Roentgen produce the x-rays which penetrated his wife's hands and left a clear impression of her bones? To understand this, we need to comprehend what happens in a cathode ray tube. This is basically a glass tube from which air has been removed. It has two electrodes: a positive electrode called an anode and a negative one called the cathode. There is also a filament which heats the cathode. When the two electrodes are connected to a source of very high voltage, the cathode accumulates a lot of negatively charged particles called electrons. These electrons evaporate because of the heat and are attracted towards the positive electrode. The stream of electrons are called cathode rays since they emanate from the cathode. When these electrons hit a phosphorescent screen, they emit a flash of light. A pattern of such flashes is what makes the images on your computer and television.

But suppose these electrons hit another piece of metal, say tungsten? The electrons, which carry a lot of energy, interact with the atoms of tungsten and give out electromagnetic radiation. If the voltage between the cathode and the anode in the cathode ray tube is appropriate, the electromagnetic rays given out are x-rays. This is what Roentgen had seen in his cathode ray tube.

We know that certain substances are opaque to visible light while others are transparent. The opaque substances cast their shadows if placed in the path of a beam of light. We see

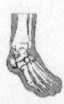

Seeing Within

this all the time around us and most dramatically when the earth casts its shadow on the moon during a lunar eclipse. In exactly the same way, certain substances are opaque to x-rays while others are transparent. Human flesh and muscle are transparent while bones are denser and hence opaque.

This is what allows your doctor to x-ray you and see if any of the bones are broken when you fall down while playing cricket and have a swollen hand. The x-ray machine in your doctor's office is basically the same as the one used by Roentgen. It is, of course, more sophisticated and allows for many other adjustments and controls in the radiation produced. The doctor asks you to put your swollen hand in front of a metal plate. The metal plate is really a light-proof container for x-ray film which is very similar to the photographic film used in your camera.

The doctor asks you to stay still and presses a button, all the time remaining behind a screen. On pressing the button, he operates the x-ray tube to produce x-rays which are focussed on to your hand. The x-rays pass right through the flesh (remember flesh is transparent to x-rays!) but are stopped by the bones. Thus, the flesh and muscle comes out lighter on the x-ray (because more x-rays have passed through them), while the bone comes as a dark shadow. The x-ray film is then developed using special chemicals just like your camera film is developed in a dark room. The doctor looks at it and bingo! There are no broken bones in your hand! So there go the dreams of missing school for several weeks.

The impact of Roentgen's discovery was immediately felt around the world. Newspaper headlines screamed 'New light sees through flesh to bones' while doctors immediately started taking pictures of bones and other parts of the body. It was very unusual for a scientific discovery to take hold of the imagination of common people in such a short time.

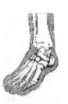

> In the initial days, any new organ that was x-rayed made newspaper headlines. In this frenzy, there were a lot of unscrupulous operators also at work. H.A. Falk in 1896 claimed to have x-rayed the human brain. His x-ray was later found to be that of a pan of cat intestines!

Some of this frenzy took on comic proportions. There were advertisements for x-ray-proof underwear and opera houses banned x-ray opera glasses for their audiences! The famous inventor Thomas Alva Edison immediately realized the importance of the discovery and started to make a hand-held x-ray lamp that could be used without any elaborate machinery. He was unsuccessful but certainly generated a lot of publicity. Studios opened which could make 'bone portraits', and poems and essays were written in praise of the new invention!

> As early as 1896, x-rays of metallic things inside purses were taken to demonstrate the penetrating power of the new radiation. Of course, there was a lot of speculation of the new technology being used for indecent things and led to many fakes like x-ray spectacles!

In this initial enthusiasm, most people did not realize the danger that exposure to this new form of light posed. Several of the enthusiasts among scientists and doctors soon saw their hair falling and lesions appearing on their skin. Though some people did warn about the harmful effects of the rays, the belief that the x-rays were harmless was so strong that they were ignored. It was not until 1904, when one of Edison's assistants who had worked with him on developing a portable x-ray machine died, that people woke up to the dangers of x-rays. It was only gradually that people started using lead screens and helmets to avoid exposure to the harmful x-rays.

Fame came almost immediately to Roentgen. He became an instant celebrity the world over. In 1901, he became the first person to get the Nobel Prize in physics for his discovery of the x-rays. Roentgen continued to live in Munich with his wife and their adopted daughter till 1919 when his wife died. Roentgen himself died in 1923 of intestinal cancer.

X-rays by then had become widespread. Even after the initial public enthusiasm had died down, the use of x-rays in medicine increased dramatically. Doctors injected various chemicals that were opaque to x-rays to study the internal organs of patients. During the World War I, the famous Polish scientist Marie Curie ran several mobile x-ray units to be able to help soldiers on the battlefield. Along with its major use in medicine, x-rays are also used extensively in scientific research nowadays. There are also many industrial uses. X-ray crystallography is a powerful technique to learn about the nature of crystals like diamond. It is also used to study the properties of various solids.

Roentgen was not only a brilliant scientist but also a very modest man. He refused offers of honorary doctorates from various universities and even rejected the offer by the government to give him a title. He donated the entire sum of the Nobel Prize money to his university for scientific research. But most importantly, he refused to patent his work so that the whole world could benefit from it.

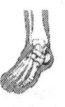

The Magical Mould

It was a Monday morning in 1928 at the Bacteriological Laboratory of the St Mary's Medical School in London. The head of the laboratory, Alexander Fleming, had just returned from a weekend vacation and it was now time to get back to work. The atmosphere in the laboratory was usually fairly chaotic because there were so many different projects going on simultaneously. And today was no different.

Fleming started to clean up by removing the petri dishes on which he had been growing colonies of bacteria. Mould had grown on some of the dishes because they had been lying over the weekend. Suddenly, Fleming noticed that on one of the dishes, the bacteria around the mould had been killed. This simple observation was to change medical science in the twentieth century and was responsible for saving countless lives. Fleming had discovered the first antibiotic, penicillin (named after the mould which came from the penicillium family), a chemical that kills bacteria. The era of antibiotics had started!

All through human history, people have been looking for ways to kill disease. Various natural agents have been used as cures. The Sumerians, around 3500 BCE, would give their patients beer with turtle shells and snakeskin. In India, ayurveda developed as a complete science of healing with thousands of herbs and chemicals prescribed for various diseases. The Chinese have a long tradition of indigenous medicine where herbs and metals play an exceedingly important role. Almost every civilization in history developed a medicine system that was effective to some extent in curing people.

> Modern doctors have found some of the amazing cures in traditional medicine systems. Acupuncture, a technique for relieving pain used for centuries in China, is widely used all over the world today. Haldi (turmeric), long known in ayurveda for its antibacterial properties, is being rediscovered by us today.
>
> Among the first traditional cure to be incorporated into modern medicine was when the European explorers found that the native Indians in South America chewed the bark of the cinchona tree to guard against malaria. While the Europeans suffered from malarial fevers in the swampy jungles, the native Indians seemed to be immune. It turned out that the bark had quinine, a chemical that is still used as a drug against malaria. An Augustinian monk in Peru described the use of this bark in curing fevers in 1633, and less than a decade later, it was in use in Europe.

By the nineteenth century, there had been major breakthroughs in medicine. Jenner had successfully used vaccination against smallpox. Pasteur had proposed the germ theory of disease—that diseases were caused by bacteria and to cure the disease, one had to kill the bacteria. As a result, many scientists were searching for chemicals that would kill the disease-causing bacteria in our bodies but were harmless to us. It was in this kind of scientific atmosphere that Fleming joined medical school.

Fleming was born in 1881 at a remote farm in rural Scotland. He was one of eight children of a farmer and spent most of his childhood on his farm, exploring nature and learning from it. After his father died, Fleming moved to London with his brother to complete his schooling, and then worked for a shipping firm for about four years. At the insistence of his brother, who was a doctor, Fleming joined medical school to start training as a surgeon.

> In 1900, during the Boer War between Britain and Southern Africa, Fleming and his two brothers joined a Scottish regiment. They spent all their time playing water polo or practising shooting but never went to Africa for the war.

Fleming was very keen on sports and was an excellent shot. When he finished medical school, he had decided to go work at another hospital. However, the captain of the shooting club at St Mary's didn't want to lose such an ace marksman and so he convinced Fleming to change over to bacteriology! And so Fleming started work at the St Mary's bacteriological department and stayed there for the rest of his life.

Around 1909, a Nobel-Prize-winning German doctor, Paul Ehrlich, was searching for a drug to cure syphilis. This dreaded disease, which was very widespread, was believed to have been introduced in Europe by the sailors returning from the Americas with Christopher Columbus. Ehrlich tried many different compounds. Finally, the 606th compound that he tried worked! Ehrlich named it salvarsan, which means that which saves by arsenic, since the medicine contained that deadly poison.

News about this great cure soon spread across Europe. Fleming was among the few doctors in London to try it on his patients. In fact, he was so successful that he was nicknamed 'Private 606'.

World War I broke out in 1914. In this devastating war, use of modern technology, including more explosive artillery and chemical weapons, meant that more people were killed and wounded than in all the other wars before—about 9,000,000 in all. Many died not in battle, but of wounds sustained in the battlefield. Most of the members of the St

The Magical Mould

Mary's bacteriology laboratory were sent to France to set up a battlefield hospital laboratory. Fleming was appalled to see that most of the wounded soldiers died of simple infections. He wondered whether one could find a chemical like salvarsan that could be effective against the bacteria causing infections.

When Fleming returned to his work at the bacteriology laboratory in London, the need for finding an antibacterial agent against infections continued to haunt him.

In 1922, he discovered that human tears contained a chemical that he called lysozyme that had antibacterial properties. This same substance is also found in albumen and body secretions. It was the first antibacterial agent found in the human body and hence was an important discovery. However, further research proved disappointing since lysozyme did not work against the stronger infections and also killed non-disease-causing bacteria.

> Not all bacteria are harmful—the curd we eat is made by bacteria which curdle the milk. In our own body, our gut has millions of bacteria, most of which aid digestion.

But this did not deter Fleming. He continued his research on antibacterial agents. In the process, he developed some very important tools for chemical analysis of drugs. He used these techniques later during his research on penicillin.

> The first person to notice the antibacterial properties of penicillium was a French medical student Ernest Duchesne. In 1896, he noticed these properties but had never reported the connection between the fungus and the antibiotic substance.

In 1928, after the accidental discovery of the antibacterial properties of the mould, Fleming worked hard to show through experiments that the mould produced a substance that could destroy the bacteria growing in the petri dishes. He extracted the penicillin and showed its effects directly on various bacteria, including one that caused deadly skin infections especially in burn patients. However, when he published his findings, the scientific community paid little attention.

Fleming soon gave up work on the mould because growing it and refining it was a very difficult process. As he was unable to produce significant quantities of penicillin, he could not conduct clinical trials on animals and humans to test the efficacy of the drug. He continued to be convinced that he had discovered a wonderful drug that could save millions of lives, but the rest of the world seemed to have forgotten about the wonderful properties of the penicillum fungus. Fleming's last published work on penicillin was in 1931.

In 1938, a team of chemists at Oxford University, which included Howard Florey and Ernst Chain, picked up Fleming's now-forgotten work on penicillin. They faced the same problems as Fleming had in purifying the chemical from the mould, but were able to purify it through some clever techniques. Their tests on animals and humans were spectacularly successful, and finally convinced scientists and doctors that Fleming had indeed found a magical counter to various infections.

Elsewhere, research on other antibacterial agents was proceeding apace. In 1932, a German scientist, Gerhard Domagk, had found that a substance derived from a dye, Prontosil, cured infections caused by the deadly streptococcus bacteria. Another antibiotic, gramicidin, was extracted from soil bacteria but it proved too toxic for human use.

In 1943, the Russian-born US-resident Selman Waksman isolated an antibiotic from soil bacteria and called it streptomycin (after the bacteria *streptomyces griseus*). This proved to be very effective against a wide range of infections but had many nasty side effects. However, it was effective against tuberculosis, also known as consumption, which had claimed millions of lives all over the world. Till the discovery of streptomycin, the only 'cure' for the disease was to go to a sanatorium in the mountains for clean air and rest.

The big boost to penicillin came after World War II broke out in 1939. Once again, thousands of soldiers were wounded and had to be treated for infections. The governments of the US and Britain collaborated to produce enough of the drug to treat soldiers, and were able to save many lives.

> During World War II, when large quantities of penicillin were needed, Florey discovered a fast-growing penicillin mould that grew on the melons sold in the supermarkets! This allowed the scientists to quickly make the huge amounts of the drug needed for soldiers.

Penicillin was still not very widely used, partly because of its high cost and difficulties in manufacturing it in sufficient quantities. Then an event happened which changed all that. There was a fire at a club in Boston in November 1942, where many people were severely burnt. Burn victims usually catch skin infections very easily because the protective outer layer of the skin is destroyed, making it easier for the bacteria to enter the body. Before the advent of penicillin, most of the deaths among burn victims were due to such infections. But this time, the American drug company Merck sent a large supply of penicillin to be used on the patients. As a result, most of them survived and penicillin was catapulted into the American national consciousness!

After the war, Fleming was recognized as a pioneer in medicine. He, along with Florey and Chain, shared the Nobel Prize for medicine in 1945.

The widespread use of penicillin, of course, saved millions of lives the world over. But because of its almost magical properties in curing previously incurable diseases, both patients and doctors used it rather carelessly. Most people, thinking of it as a miracle drug, would take large quantities of it even for non-bacterial diseases! This had disastrous effects, which had been predicted by Fleming himself. Several of the bacteria became antibiotic resistant.

Bacteria are organisms that reproduce at a very fast rate. When a person takes less than a full dose of an antibiotic, only some of the bacteria die. Those that remain are obviously more suited for fighting the antibiotic since they have survived. In time, these reproduce and their offspring inherit this resistance. The end result of this is that the bacteria that could be treated with a particular antibiotic previously become resistant to it. We have seen this happen in our own times where the deadly bacteria which causes tuberculosis has become resistant to most of the medicines used for it.

Fleming died in 1955 and was buried in St Paul's Cathedral in London. Scientists have discovered over thirty different antibiotics to date. Some of them work very well with certain kinds of bacteria while others work against a whole range of infections. These are called broad-spectrum antibiotics. So the next time you go to a doctor with a chest infection and he prescribes an antibiotic which cures you, you can thank the slimy, white fungus which made it all possible! And of course, you should also remember Alexander Fleming who saw the potential of the mould to make the lives of millions of people healthier.

The Particles of Life

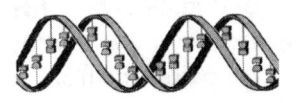

The last day of February 1953 was a cold day in Cambridge. At lunchtime, two young scientists walked briskly into the Eagle, a pub on Benet Street, to celebrate a hard morning's work. After settling down with a drink, the older of the two, Francis Crick announced to the people gathered at the pub, 'We have found the secret of life'! And indeed that morning Crick and James Watson had just made the most important discovery in biology—they had unveiled the structure of the DNA molecule. In discovering the structure of the molecule responsible for transmission of hereditary information, they had answered one of the most important questions in science.

The idea that a single chemical molecule could hold all the information needed for a living thing seemed absurd till about a hundred years ago. Before Darwin proposed his theory of evolution, it was believed that life, in all its wonderful diversity and detail, was exactly as it had been designed by a creator. The idea that a complicated thing like a human being could arise by natural causes seemed as absurd then as the idea of an old woman on the moon today! Darwin showed that small changes over thousands of generations could lead to the complexity of life that we see today. Natural selection was the engine of change, and changes accumulated over generations led to life forms being the way they were. But the key question still remained: what exactly was the mechanism of heredity? Where and how is the information to pass on to the next generation stored?

Around the same time as Darwin, an Austrian monk, Gregor Mendel (1822–84), was trying to find the answers to these questions. Mendel worked with flowering pea plants and studied their characteristics over many generations. What he found was that the characteristics were inherited as units (in pairs, one from each parent) and that each of these units were passed on independent of others. We now call these units genes.

Mendel's work was largely unknown for several decades. It was only in the early 1900s that several biologists started taking note of it. One such scientist was the American Thomas Morgan who experimented with the fruit fly. What Morgan found was that the location of a gene (the thing responsible for inheriting the characteristics from the parents) could be identified with certain areas of the chromosome. Chromosomes are thin strands of genetic material that the biologists had already located in the nucleus of the cells. They copy themselves and separate. But how exactly the genetic information passed from the old to the new was still a mystery.

> Fruit flies are the favourite subjects for geneticists to study because they reproduce very fast. Many generations can be studied in a matter of a few months.

Over the next few decades, several biologists worked on the problem of trying to locate precisely where and how the genetic information is stored. By the mid 1940s, it was established that a molecule called DNA (deoxyribonucleic acid) was responsible for the transmission of genetic traits. But two key questions remained unanswered. What was the structure of DNA? And how does it pass on the genetic information between generations?

This was the situation in 1950 when Crick, a thirty-four-year-old Englishman, rejoined Cambridge University to finish his PhD in physics. He had started in 1939, but his research was interrupted by World War II, during which he worked as a scientist in the Admiralty. In 1951, he met a young American James Watson who had joined Cambridge as a research scholar. Watson and Crick soon realized that they shared a common interest in trying to unravel the mystery of life by understanding the structure of the DNA molecule. They started working together.

The two men came from very different backgrounds. Crick, born in 1916, was the son of a shoe factory owner in Northampton, England. He studied in Northampton and London and got his BSc. degree from London in 1937, before embarking on his PhD.

Watson was born in 1928 in Chicago. His parents were of English and Scottish descent, and his father was a businessman in Chicago. Watson got his early education in Chicago and completed his bachelor's degree in zoology in 1947. He had a passion for bird watching: as a child, he would spend hours trying to learn about birds and their habitats. This interest in birds finally matured into a desire to learn genetics. He finished a PhD in zoology from Indiana University in 1950. After some research at laboratories in Europe, he joined Cambridge to pursue research in genetics.

> Watson used to spend a lot of his time reading the world almanac, and once won $100 as a prize in a radio quiz programme. He bought binoculars with the money so that he could watch birds!

At the Cavendish Laboratory in Cambridge, where Watson and Crick worked, most people were interested in the structure of proteins. These are molecules that play a crucial role in the chemistry of life, though they have little role in the passing on of inherited traits. Most of the work on DNA was going on at another laboratory in King's College, London, under the supervision of Maurice Wilkins and Rosalind Franklin.

Wilkins and Franklin were studying the structure of DNA and other molecules using a technique called x-ray diffraction. In this technique, x-rays were used to study crystals of substances. The pattern of bright and dark spots, obtained when the x-rays pass through the crystals, tells us about the arrangement of the atoms in the crystal. What they had determined so far was that the DNA molecule had a peculiar structure.

Franklin had been taking x-ray pictures of the DNA molecule for some time now. Born in 1920 in London, she was trained as a chemist. She joined King's College in 1951 and started working on the DNA molecule. Those days there were very few women in science. Male scientists did not take Franklin's work seriously, neither did Wilkins. But hostility from her colleagues did not deter Franklin and she continued her research. From several x-ray photographs taken in 1951, Franklin was convinced that the DNA molecule had a helical structure, which means like a spiral staircase, which curves and moves forward too.

In 1952, Franklin took the famous Photo 51 which clearly showed the double helix or twisted staircase structure of the DNA molecule. But, as luck would have it, she filed the picture away because there was an earlier, hazier picture on which she was working at that time.

Around this time, Watson visited Wilkins at King's College who showed him Franklin's Photo 51. This was done without Franklin's permission, and some people think that Wilkins did it deliberately. On the train ride back to Cambridge, Watson made a sketch of the photograph from memory. On his return, he shared with Crick what he had seen in the photographs. This was all the inspiration that the two of them needed.

For several months, both scientists had been making

The Particles of Life

models of the DNA molecule with cardboard and sticks. None of the several structures they tried out seemed to agree with all that was known about the molecule from the x-ray pictures and other studies.

And then, finally, on 28 February 1953, it all fell into place. Not only did they finally make sense of how all the different elements fitted together into a neat structure but they also comprehended how the structure made possible the passing of genetic traits between generations.

How does it all work? Let us start with the cell. The cell, which is the basic structure of life, has—among other things—chromosomes in its nucleus. Chromosomes are the structures that carry the genetic information. This information is organized on the chromosomes in the form of DNA. DNA is the genetic material of most living things on our planet.

A molecule of DNA has long strands of chemicals, called nucleotides, which are linked to form two chains. The chains are arranged like a twisted ladder and this is called a double helix. The nucleotide is made up of three components—a kind of sugar called deoxyribose, a phosphate and one of four chemicals called bases. These four bases—adenine, guanine, thymine and cystosine—make up what is called the alphabet of life. We will call them A, G, T and C.

How do these form a helix? The nucleotide has the sugar molecule in the centre and the phosphate on one side and the base on the other. The phosphate also links to the sugar molecule of the next nucleotide, thus forming the parallel rails of the ladder. The bases face inwards towards the centre of the ladder.

Imagine two such chains of nucleotides as ladders facing each other. The rails are made up of alternate sugar and phosphate molecules. But what about the rungs? It turns out that some of the bases have a special liking for each other. Thus, the A base likes to be with the T base, and the G base with the C base. In this way, the base A on one nucleotide

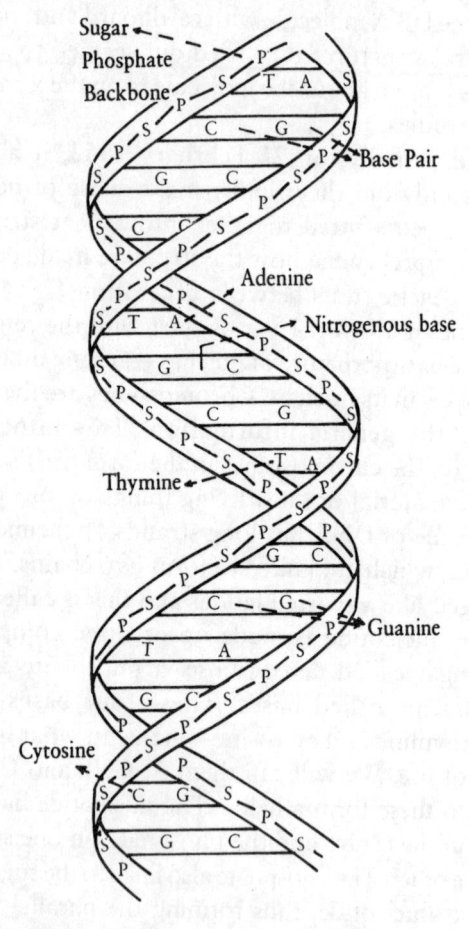

Schematic Diagram of DNA Structure

links up with base T of the nucleotide on the facing rail. In scientific terms, these two bases form a bond. These bases are called complimentary, i.e., A is complementary to T, and C to G.

Thus we have two rails of alternating sugar and phosphate

units with the rungs made up of A-T or C-G pairs. The whole thing is twisted like a rope ladder.

This ladder is the fundamental building block of all life that we know of. The sequence of the nucleotides determines the structure of the gene. The sequence of these letters along the DNA is what makes up the genetic make-up of all living things. This genetic sequence is read by other molecules (called RNA) to manufacture proteins. Proteins are the molecules that regulate and determine the functioning of the cell, and hence of the organism as a whole.

But how does this twisted ladder structure work to pass on the genetic traits?

The first thing to note is that when the cell divides, it needs to pass on the DNA to the daughter cell. The process of the DNA molecule copying itself for each descendant is called replication. What happens is that the twisted ladder breaks off along the centre, leaving the two chains of nucleotides. In each of these chains, the nucleotides attract the complementary nucleotides that are floating around in the cell and form another double helix. A particular nucleotide will only bond with a complementary one. The new double helix is an exact copy of the old one. In this way, the structure of the DNA is passed on from generation to generation.

Watson and Crick announced their discovery to the scientific community in 1953. Franklin and Wilkins also published their findings together with Watson and Crick. The structure was so elegant and obvious that it was instantly accepted by biologists. The breakthrough was just what biologists had been waiting for. The field of molecular biology and genetics grew very fast in a few years. Watson, Crick and Wilkins got the Nobel Prize for medicine in 1962, four years after Franklin's death from cancer.

> In his memoir *What Mad Pursuit*, Crick wrote that 'rather than believe that Watson and Crick made the DNA structure, I would rather stress that the structure made Watson and Crick'.

By this time, Watson and Crick had gone their separate ways. Watson went to work at Harvard University and finally became the director of the Cold Spring Harbor Lab in the US. He played an important part in the Human Genome Project recently. The Human Genome Project was one of the most ambitious tasks undertaken by scientists. Its purpose was to decipher the entire DNA of humans, i.e. to find out the sequence of the nucleotides in the DNA. With the aid of new techniques and computers, hundreds of scientists around the world collaborated on this. The information obtained will prove to be of great use in our understanding of life. It will also be useful for developing new drugs.

Crick continued working in England till 1976, when he moved to the Salk Institute in the US. He died in 2003.

> Crick's house in Cambridge, the Portugal Place, had a golden double helix above the front door.

Finding the double helical structure of the DNA molecule has been compared to finding the Holy Grail of biology. Once this was understood, progress was rapid. In less than fifty years, we have a developed science of biotechnology where scientists manipulate the genes to produce drugs, chemicals and even better varieties of crops. The discovery of Watson and Crick (together with Wilkins and Franklin) opened up the new frontiers of knowledge—knowledge that may well shape the twenty-first century.